CONTRI

(In Or

Kye Sun Rose
LoveWarriorProject.com

Christine Naluzze
ChristineNaluzze.com

Barbara Magro Berg
TheScienceofAttractingYourSoulmate.com

Mary Jane Charles
LastWishesnNSupport.com

Pastor Dr. Dorothy Ross
DorothyRoss.com

Audrey Kirwin
TheCrisisPlanners.com

Robin Tasco
RobinTasco.com

Beverly Brooke Peterson
LadyRejuvenator.com

Dawn McCarter
DawnMcCarter.com

Diana Spirithawk
DianasSpirithawk.com

Maureen Cohen
MaureenCohen.com

Lisa Baker
Ascentim.com

Being The One

How to Lead Boldly & Live Your Vision

Volume II

Praise for Being The One - Volume II

"An exquisite reminder of how powerful we truly are, even in moments when we feel anything but."

~ Kelly Sullivan Walden

"A treasure trove of inspiration."

~ Phyliss Ireland

"What a great compilation of stories that are inspiring and easy to grasp!"

~ Le

"This book has solid and loving advice to help anyone be their best self."

~ Janet Conlon

"These stories are honest, uplifting, and deeply motivating. If you're ready to take inspired action, this book will light a fire in you. It did in me!"

~ Martin Cohen

Being The One

How to Lead Boldly & Live Your Vision

Volume II

Insights & Inspiration
From 13 Visionary Leaders

Nancy Matthews

Published with the collaboration of Courageous Women Publications™.

Cover credit, Nancy Matthews.

Nancy Matthews
Plantation, Florida 33324
(954) 710-6900
https://NancyMatthews.com

ISBN: 979-8-9997282-2-7 (eBook)
ISBN: 979-8-9997282-3-4 (paperback)

Limits of Liability and Disclaimer of Warranty

The author and publisher shall not be liable for your misuse of this material. This book is strictly for informational and educational purposes.

Warning–Disclaimer

The purpose of this book is to educate and entertain. The author and/or publisher do not guarantee that anyone following these techniques, suggestions, tips, ideas, or strategies will become successful. The author and/or publisher shall have neither liability nor responsibility to anyone with respect to any loss or damage caused, or alleged to be caused, directly or indirectly by the information contained in this book.

Dedicated to every person
who senses there is more within them,
and who is brave enough
to become The One who brings it to life.

Table of Contents

Introduction xii

Section 1

Remembering & Reclaiming 1

Chapter 1 - Remembering Your True Self: Follow Your Happy

Kye Sun Rose 3

Chapter 2 - Made for More: Reclaiming Identity, Power & Purpose from the Inside Out

Christine Naluzze. 13

Chapter 3 - Stepping From 'Impossible' Into 'I'm Possible': Being The One For Myself Who Attracts Lasting Love

Barbara Magro Berg 22

Chapter 4 - The Thread That Pulled Me Here

Mary Jane ("MJ") Charles 31

Section 2

Faith, Courage & Becoming 41

Chapter 5 - Praying for the Impossible: Activating Mountain-Moving Faith

Pastor Dr. Dorothy Ross 43

Chapter 6 - The Bold Approach to Your Life's Journey with a Plan to Survive & Thrive

Audrey Kirwin 51

Chapter 7 -From Shell to Sanctuary:The First Quad That Built Me

Robin Tasco 60

Chapter 8 - It's Never Too Late to Rejuvenate
Beverly Brooke Peterson. 69

SECTION 3

LIVING & LEADING AS THE ONE.............................. 77

Chapter 9 - Seeing The One
Dawn McCarter 79

Chapter 10 - Soul Medicine Arts: Remembering The Sacred Ways of Being The One
Dr. Diana Spirithawk, DSS 87

Chapter 11 - Becoming Financially Free: Coming Home to Myself
Maureen Cohen 95

Chapter 12 - Bold Moves, Brave Faith: My Journey from Success to Significance
Lisa L. Baker. 103

CONCLUSION 111

ACKNOWLEDGMENTS 113

CONTINUE YOUR JOURNEY.................................114

ABOUT NANCY MATTHEWS 116

Introduction

The Journey of Being The One

There are moments in life when something within us begins to stir.

Sometimes it arrives as a whisper, an uneasy feeling that the life we are living is only a fraction of the life we are meant to lead. Sometimes it arrives as a disruption, a turning point that forces us to question who we are, what we believe, and what truly matters.

I can recall many such moments in my life and the times when I took action to follow the inspiration of those moments, as well as the times I did not. While I firmly believe in living with no regrets about the times I did not follow the call, there is strong evidence that shows when I have taken inspired action, listening to that whisper (which has occasionally been a loud roar), my experiences have been more fulfilling, rewarding, and, quite frankly, fun!

- The moment I discovered I was pregnant, single, and in no way ready to become a mother, yet the voice inside said, "You can give this child a good life."
- The moment I quit my job at the law firm to venture out on my own.
- The moment I said yes to co-create a company designed for women business owners to connect, grow, and prosper.
- The moment the essence and message of "The One Philosophy" emerged from my spirit.

What about the moments where I did not take action? Rather than seeing those as mistakes, I look to them to explore what may have held me back from taking action, what lesson I needed to learn in the unfolding of my calling, and what I can glean from that action to respond differently now and in the future.

All of these moments changed the trajectory of my life, leading me to the continuous fulfilment of my purpose and calling... in Being The One.

Being The One is not about perfection, status, or achievement. It is about responsibility, the quiet yet powerful choice, moment by moment to listen to the whispers—the voice within that comes from above, guiding you to play out your role in the wildly complex fabric of life.

When we live this way, leadership becomes less about authority and more about presence. Influence becomes less about control and more about connection. And success becomes not only what we accomplish, but who we become.

This book is a collection of stories from individuals who have stepped onto that path.

Each author shares a deeply personal journey, moments of rediscovery, faith, courage, reinvention, and alignment. Their stories remind us that transformation rarely happens in a straight line. It unfolds through challenges, unexpected opportunities, courageous choices, and the willingness to listen to the deeper wisdom within.

Together, their experiences reveal a powerful truth: the path to leading boldly and living your vision begins inside.

The chapters in this book unfold through three interconnected movements, three expressions of the same essence. Think of them as a trinity that reflects the natural evolution of personal and purposeful leadership.

Remembering & Reclaiming invites us to return to ourselves. It is the moment we recognize that parts of our identity, our joy, or our voice may have been buried beneath expectations, disappointments, or life's responsibilities. Here we rediscover the truth of who we are.

Faith, Courage & Becoming is the stage where transformation takes shape. It is where belief grows stronger than fear and where bold action begins to replace hesitation. In this space, we stretch beyond what once seemed possible.

Living & Leading as The One represents embodiment. It is where the philosophy moves from idea to lived experience. Leadership becomes an expression of alignment, service, and purpose. When we reach this stage, our lives become an invitation for others to rise as well.

Although these sections appear as separate parts of the book, they are not separate journeys. They are facets of the same unfolding truth.

Remembering leads to becoming.
Becoming leads to living.
And living as The One inspires others to do the same.

The stories that follow are not meant to place these authors on a pedestal. Instead, they offer a mirror, a reminder that the courage, wisdom, and potential you admire in others already exists within you.

The question is not whether the world needs more leaders.

The question is whether you are answering the call and Being The One.

A Moment for Reflection

Before you turn the page and begin the stories in this book, take a quiet moment to reflect.

Every journey of transformation begins with a simple question: What is stirring within me right now?
As you read the chapters that follow, you may see pieces of your own life reflected in the experiences of these authors, their turning points, their courage, their doubts, and their breakthroughs. Their stories are not meant to be admired from a distance. They are meant to awaken something within you.

Consider these questions as you begin:

- What part of my life is calling for greater courage or truth right now?
- Where might I be ready to reclaim a deeper part of who I am?
- What vision, dream, or possibility is waiting for me to step forward and claim it?
- What might change if I chose to show up as The One in my life today?

You do not need all the answers before you begin. Take the questions with you as you delve into the stories of these brilliant authors.

Sometimes the most powerful transformation starts with a single moment of awareness and the willingness to take the next step.

Turn the page and let the journey unfold.

With Love & Light,
Nancy Matthews
Creator of The One Philosophy

Section 1

Remembering & Reclaiming

Every meaningful change in our lives begins with a moment of awareness.

Sometimes it arrives as a whisper, the quiet recognition that something within us has been waiting to be acknowledged. Sometimes it comes through life experiences that invite us to pause and reconsider who we are, what we believe, and what truly matters.

In the busyness of everyday life, it is easy to lose sight of pieces of ourselves. Our dreams may become buried beneath responsibilities. Our voices may soften beneath expectations. Yet the truth of who we are never disappears. It simply waits to be remembered.

The stories in this section reflect those moments of awakening. Moments when these authors recognized a deeper calling within themselves and began the journey of reclaiming their identity, their purpose, and their voice.

Remembering & Reclaiming is the beginning of Being The One. It is the sacred return to yourself, where you reconnect with the truth that has always been there, waiting for you to notice.

Chapter 1

Remembering Your True Self: Follow Your Happy

Kye Sun Rose
Founder, Love Warrior Project

Remembering Your True Self: Follow Your Happy

My Vision & Mission: Returning to the Heart

From as far back as I can remember, there was an undeniable knowing inside me—a pull toward healing that didn't need explanation. I couldn't have described it as intuition or energy back then, but I felt things deeply. When someone was hurting, I sensed it and wanted to do something about it. Healing others felt natural, instinctive. It was simply part of who I was.

Still, when it came time to choose a career path, practicality outweighed intuition. I considered medical school from an early age, but ultimately chose a different route. Even though I had an intense desire to apply to medical school, I had an undeniable sense that this path would rob me of experiencing joy in my life. This inner guidance was so strong that I made a tough decision, made a course correction in my life, and chose a career as a Physician Assistant. This path felt right, and I found the training to be easy and fun. I found joy in helping people and, ultimately, happiness in learning Dermatology, a pursuit that lasted twenty-six years.

It seemed a stable and meaningful way to help people. For many years, that decision made sense. I was successful, respected, and fully immersed in the work. I enjoyed caring for my patients and supporting them—not just medically, but emotionally.

Yet even within that success, there was a quiet, persistent sense that something deeper was waiting for me.

That more profound truth began to surface in the most unexpected—and painful—way when I was thirty-eight. I decided to have a baby with someone I was not aligned with. It was not the kind of committed partnership that comes with having a child together. It wasn't a relationship built on shared values or a sustainable future, and on some level, I knew that. But I ignored the signs, convinced myself it would work, and kept going. That decision brought me to a place I never expected: a deep depression that forced me to confront what I had been avoiding. At first, the heaviness felt like failure. But with time, I began to see it for what it really was, a much-needed course correction. The lack of joy, the emotional suffering, was a message for me to take notice. A moment of intervention from something greater than myself, saying, "Stop. Look deeper. This path is not your truth."

As painful as it was, that depression cracked something open inside me. It initiated a search that was not intellectual but spiritual. It pushed me toward the healing work I had avoided for years. I began exploring therapy, and not long after, I entered the world of Lakota ceremony. The moment I stepped into my first Sweat Lodge, everything shifted. Something ancient and familiar awakened within me. The songs, the prayers, the heat, the intention—it brought me back to a version of myself I forgot existed.

The ceremonies of Vision Quest, Sundance, and carrying the Pipe were not just experiences; they were initiations and a remembering. They helped me peel back the layers that had been covering my True Self. They showed me that healing wasn't just something I could do—it was who I had always been. I now look back and remember there was joy in every moment partaking in the ceremonies.

But Earth School has a way of testing our alignment, even after profound awakening. As I continued to grow spiritually, I also felt a desire for greater personal freedom—for my time, my finances, and my purpose. I wanted to serve in bigger ways and live with more autonomy.

That desire led me into Beachbody coaching. Several people close to me, especially those in my spiritual circle, were having incredible success. They entered the millionaire club, bought homes, and transformed their lives. I applied myself fully, did everything I was "supposed" to do, and expected similar results. But that path didn't open for me the way it opened for others. I was miserable.

At first, I blamed myself, thinking I wasn't trying hard enough or was missing something. But eventually, I realized the truth: it wasn't a match for my soul. Joy was missing from the whole experience. The misalignment created resistance. The resistance created friction. And once again, life was nudging me toward another course correction.

That redirection brought me to coaching, energy medicine, and more healing. Helping others grow, develop, and step into their highest potential could be the combination of purpose and freedom I was seeking. I joined programs, pursued training, and tried to mold myself into a traditional coach. Yet the discomfort returned. The intuitive "no" I had felt before resurfaced, yet it was stronger. Something about this path felt forced, and it wasn't enjoyable. My intuition grew louder, clearer: "This isn't it either. Keep going."

What finally changed everything was the moment I stepped fully into energetic healing—not just as a student, but as a practitioner. Following the nudge to focus on healing transformed me. It felt right, I thought I was on the right course. I finally realized that my intuition was always correct and consistently shifted my confusion, frustration, and sadness toward what made me happy. The healing modalities I trained in allowed me to release emotions and old patterns, and through a Divine partnership I had created along the way, catapulted my results to a new level. My divinely guided healing helped me overcome procrastination, self-doubt, overwhelm, and the internal blocks that had made abundance and financial freedom feel impossible.

The sudden death of my spiritual teacher hit me hard, and in that pain, I found the courage to leave my medical practice of thirty-one years and start my healing business. I was compelled to step fully into my purpose and my dream; it was now or never. This decision was the hardest of all the course corrections to make. The fear of failure, the anxiety around starting a business from scratch, and the prospect of doing it all on my own were overwhelming. I was guided to trust. Trust in my intuition. Trust in my divine guidance. Trust in my True Self. This move allowed me to relocate to my horse farm in the South, out of the cold, and my dream for my retirement suddenly came true.

For the first time, I saw and felt my True Self clearly. And with that clarity came an amazingly effective tool for healing: The Body Code. When I combined Body Code work with the Divine energies, the results were extraordinary—not just for me, but for others as well.

Emotions that had been buried for decades began to release.
Beliefs that had held people hostage unraveled with ease.
Physical symptoms diminished and then disappeared.
People began remembering themselves.

This wasn't traditional coaching.
This wasn't therapy.
This wasn't mindset work.
This was healing at the level of truth.

And that's when the real alignment happened: I loved the process. I found it effortless and joyful. My business blossomed and grew. Slowly and consistently, it sustained me and helped me thrive. I became an international healer and spiritual coach—not by chasing a title, but by following my soul.

People began finding me; they came seeking clarity, relief, connection, and purpose. And session after session, ceremony after ceremony, the same insight became undeniable:

Our suffering doesn't come from who we are.
It comes from who we think we have to be.

Every trapped emotion
Every limiting belief
Every internalized story
Every inherited pattern
Every layer of conditioning
Covers the light of our True Self.

My entire journey, every misstep, every redirection, every moment of doubt, taught me that our purpose here is not to perfect ourselves. It is to uncover ourselves, to remember ourselves.

To unveil the truth beneath the layers. To remember what we've forgotten. To shed what never belonged to us in the first place.

I now understand that the path of the Healer is not discovered in a single moment. It is revealed through a long becoming—a gradual alignment with the truth we carried before we ever arrived on Earth.

My journey began with a childhood knowing and moved through decades of medical service, cracked open through emotional collapse, deepened through ceremony, pivoted through misalignment, accelerated through Divine partnership, and ultimately led me back to the Healer I have always been.

Today, as an international healer and spiritual coach, my work is grounded in one simple mission: Helping others uncover their True Self by releasing the suffering—physical, emotional, mental, and spiritual—that dims their light.

I don't see people as broken.
I don't see them as lost.
I see them as layered.

And layer by layer, emotion by emotion, belief by belief, I help them return to the truth beneath it all:

They are a unique expression of the Divine.
They are light.
They are love.
They are whole.

This is the purpose of Earth School.
Not to reinvent ourselves—
But to remember ourselves.
And when we do, the world transforms with us.

Tools That Reveal Your True Self

Healing and awakening are not random events; they are processes rooted in intention, devotion, and Divine partnership. Along my own journey—and through guiding others—several key strategies emerged as powerful catalysts for transformation.

1. **Listen to the Whisper Before It Becomes a Scream.**
   Your True Self speaks softly at first. It nudges, nudges again, then pulls harder.
   When you ignore it, the universe amplifies the message.

Learning to listen early—through meditation, intuition, and body awareness—prevents unnecessary suffering.
Exercise:
Take three minutes daily to ask:
"What is my soul trying to tell me today?"
Write the first thing that comes. Do not edit. Do not judge.

2. **Invite the Divine In.**
   Every session I facilitate begins with a simple yet profound intention:
   "Divine, take the lead."
   Healing does not come from me; it flows through me. The same is true for every person. When you invite the Divine into your healing, transformation happens faster, more gently, and more completely.
3. **Work With the Higher Self.**
   We each carry an inner compass—our Higher Self—that knows the path, the purpose, and the truth. When I began consciously connecting to my Higher Self and my clients' Higher Selves, the healing became precise, efficient, and filled with grace.

   Exercise:

   Sit quietly, place a hand over your heart, and say:
   "Higher Self, guide me. Show me what I am ready to release."
   Notice what arises. Give what arises attention and invite it to release, thanking it for the message and the experience. This could be anxiety, sadness, panic... any emotion. It can feel like a tension, a heaviness. The mere act of focusing on the sensation allows what needs to be released from your energy system.
4. **Learn the Body's Language.**
   Experience the Emotion Code/Body Code/Belief Code, which opens a portal to understanding the body's intelligence. Emotions that are not processed become lodged in the body—creating pain, anxiety, depression, fatigue, and disconnection from purpose.

When we release these trapped energies, the True Self shines through like sunlight breaking through clouds.

5. **Ceremony Heals in Ways Nothing Else Can.**
Courage, surrender, connection—these qualities are forged in ceremony. Whether through Sweat Lodge, Vision Quest, Sundance, or My Spirit Horse Healing Pipe Ceremony, I have shared sacred ritual with others for twenty-seven years, bringing us into direct communion with the Divine.

Healing in Action

One of the most profound demonstrations of Divine guidance occurred during the pandemic. As fear and separation spread across the world, I felt called to support my community through ceremony—not once, not twice, but every single night for a hundred consecutive nights, we gathered in prayer, song, and sacred connection. People from all walks of life joined: empaths overwhelmed by the collective emotion, healers unable to serve in their usual ways, parents burdened with anxiety, and individuals facing deep loneliness.

Night after night, something miraculous happened. Hearts softened. Tears were released. Old emotional wounds dissolved. People began to reconnect with hope, peace, and their own Divinity.

One woman, an empath who had suffered from debilitating anxiety for years, experienced a breakthrough on night thirty-seven.

Through the combination of ceremony, EFT, and Divine energy work, she finally released the emotional block that had been holding her hostage. Today, she leads her own circles—a Love Warrior in every sense of the word.

Another client—a high-performing business executive—came to me riddled with burnout, self-doubt, and physical tension. Within weeks of working with the Body Code sessions, he reconnected with his purpose, revitalized his leadership, and began inspiring others through compassion rather than fear.

Every story, every transformation, every life touched reaffirmed the message I had resisted for so long:

This profound work is what I was born to do.

Your Path to Becoming a Love Warrior

The journey to discovering your True Self does not begin with trying harder; It starts with a single choice:

To say yes to love, yes to healing, and yes to your soul's purpose by following what brings you joy.

Visit LoveWarriorProject.com and receive my free video: *Heart Centered Breath Process.*

I invite you to become a Love Warrior—someone who leads with compassion, lives with intention, and walks with the Divine.

Here are three ways to begin:

1. **Daily Heart Alignment.**
   Place your hands on your heart and breathe in the energy of love.
   Ask: "What would love have me do today?"
2. **Release What No Longer Serves You.**
   Make an appointment with me to experience the Emotion Code/Body Code to release stored emotional blocks. Lightness creates clarity.
3. **Connect With Me Personally.**
   If you feel called to deepen your journey, work with me directly through private sessions, ceremonies, or the Love Warrior Project.

Together, we will create a life—and a world—guided by love, powered by grace, and aligned with the Divine.

Kye Sun Rose is a Spiritual Coach, Energy Healer, and founder of the Love Warrior Project, a heart-centered movement empowering people to transcend suffering and live from love, compassion, kindness, and gratitude. After over 30 years as a Physician Assistant, Kye answered her lifelong calling to heal through the Divine, blending science with sacred ceremony.

Rooted in the Lakota traditions since 1998, she leads the Spirit Horse Healing Pipe Ceremony, guiding others in prayer, sacred song, and drumming for profound transformation. A Reiki Master, Golden Light Healer, Body Code Practitioner, Evolutionary Mystic Meditation Facilitator, and Ignite Your Power Coach, Kye channels Divine energy and connects with each client's Higher Self to restore balance and awaken their True Essence.

Through her work, Kye helps empaths, healers, and high performers release pain, dissolve limiting beliefs, and rediscover their innate wholeness. A co-author in Inspired Living and Love Warriors, she invites all to walk the path of Oneness—where healing, purpose, and joy flow freely, and every heart becomes a Love Warrior.

Visit LoveWarriorProject.com and receive a free video: "Heart Centered Breath Process."

LoveWarriorProject.com
Kye@LoveWarriorProject.com

Chapter 2

Made for More: Reclaiming Identity, Power & Purpose from the Inside Out

Christine Naluzze

Transformational Strategist
Author & Speaker

Made for More: Reclaiming Identity, Power & Purpose from the Inside Out

I have lived the pain of identity loss and the power of identity awakening. I know what it means to arrive in a new country labeled an immigrant, a single mother, and yet hear God say, "You are more." My drive comes from witnessing how confusion about who we are keeps us small, settling, surviving, and shrinking our gifts in silence.

I have walked through the journey of breaking patterns, finding purpose, and discovering that true transformation doesn't start with business, confidence, or skill. It begins with identity. I am driven to guide women into alignment because I've seen firsthand how identity becomes the turning point—from lack to legacy, from pain to purpose, from being overlooked to becoming ordained to lead.

I lead because this is not something I studied—it's something I survived, transformed, and now carry as a mantle for others.

I made a decision to be the one—to live boldly in my identity, stand in my God-given purpose, and shine as a vessel of love and light. I chose to lead by example, showing what it looks like to break patterns, build a purposeful life, and live from alignment, not fear or survival.

It matters to others because every woman carries a vision inside her, but many are waiting for permission they don't realize they already have. When one woman rises in confidence and identity, she becomes a mirror of possibility for others. She shifts her lineage, influences her community, and becomes a catalyst for generational change.

This message matters because we are not waiting for someone else to lead; we are called to be The One to lead.

I didn't discover this vision in a moment of success. I found it in a season of exhaustion. For years, I gave myself away to survival, working long hours, missing weekends, forfeiting rest, chasing stability, and sacrificing connection. I kept believing that working harder would eventually lead to peace, freedom, and a better life for my family.

But instead of gaining more, I kept losing pieces of myself.

I chased every "shiny" opportunity that promised escape from the rat race. I tried business ideas out of desperation, not alignment. I invested money I barely had, hoping one of them would be the breakthrough I needed. Yet everything seemed to cost more of me than it gave back. The stress, burnout, and constant striving left me empty, working endlessly but never actually living.

Then, in that tired place, a question grew louder:

"Isn't there more?"

Another whisper followed:

"If others can live free, why not you?"

At first, I resisted. My mind was filled with patterns of scarcity, fear, and beliefs formed from years of just trying to survive. But the voice didn't go away—it grew clearer.

And I realized I wasn't being called to chase the next opportunity...

I was being called to transform.
To pause.
To unlearn.
To align.

The moment I stopped working only for a living and started working for a life, that's when my vision came into focus.

I understood that freedom, fulfillment, and purpose don't come from hustle. They come from identity, clarity, and alignment with who God created us to be.

That was the turning point.
Not when I finally earned more—
But when I finally believed...
I am made for more.

One of the greatest challenges in becoming "The One" was learning to stand confidently in my identity—even in seasons with no applause, no visible results, and no external proof that my voice mattered.

In the beginning, I stepped into rooms where women were already established. They had clarity, influence, confidence, and resources. I admired them deeply, yet their boldness confronted the insecurities I hadn't yet faced in myself. I questioned whether I belonged, whether I had anything valuable to offer, and whether I could lead the way I felt called to.

With time, I discovered that the real challenge was not a lack of resources, it was the inner battle with fear, scarcity, and self-doubt. I had to learn that identity is tested long before it is celebrated, and purpose requires us to believe before we see, to move before we feel ready, and to remain faithful even when nothing seems to be working.

A defining turning point came when I wrote my first book, ***Strength for Tough Times***. Writing it demanded courage—I worried who would read it, how it would be received, and whether my voice mattered beyond my own story. But I wrote it anyway because I believed there was purpose in my pain and hope in my testimony.

Soon after, I launched my first program, Impact Accelerator, a "5-Day Idea to Income" experience. I poured everything into it—late nights, effort, strategy, prayer, and belief. Yet when it ended without a single person signing up, the silence was heavy. It would have been easy to retreat, shrink back, or question whether I was truly made for more.

But instead, something shifted.

I chose not to abandon my calling just because the results weren't immediate. I realized that leadership is not proven by applause; it is proven by courage and obedience. I stopped waiting for a breakthrough to validate my purpose and began honoring the purpose itself.

That was my breakthrough:

I stopped waiting to be seen and started choosing to become.

Not the woman who succeeds quickly,
but the woman who leads faithfully.
Not the woman who waits for proof,
but the woman who trusts the call.

This journey reminds me of Jesus' words: "I am the True Vine, and you are the branches." Each branch bears fruit not by competition, but by connection—by abiding. Just as branches don't fight for sunlight, I learned I didn't need to strive to measure up to others. I simply needed to grow where God planted me and produce the fruit aligned with my calling.

My struggles were not failures; they were pruning. They strengthened my character, deepened my faith, and taught me that a woman called for more is not called only to rise—she is called to lift. We bear fruit not just for ourselves, but to nourish others, to multiply impact, and to demonstrate the fullness of what God can do through a life aligned with purpose.

Dawn's Story

When I talk about what it means to be The One, I don't speak from theory. I've watched this truth unfold in the real lives of women I've been privileged to serve. One of them is Dawn, whom I've walked alongside for over a decade. Her story reflects what this book calls every woman into: living boldly and living her vision.

When we first connected, Dawn was full of potential but uncertain of her direction. She wanted to make a difference, but she wrestled with fear, identity, and the weight of expectations. She questioned whether she could lead, whether her voice mattered, and whether her desire to help others was enough to build a purpose-driven life.

Over the years, I never pushed her to chase success quickly or rush into opportunities for visibility. Instead, I stood beside her and called out the woman she was becoming. Together, we unpacked clarity, spiritual alignment, confidence, and identity. We prayed, strategized, and aligned her decisions with purpose, not pressure.

And Dawn learned something powerful:

Leadership is not found in titles; it is formed through identity. Success is not something you chase; it is something you step into when you build a life rooted in who God says you are.

Today, Dawn is a Clinical Mental Health Counselor, a mother, a wife, and a leader who serves from wholeness. She didn't just reach a career goal—she became a woman capable of stewarding impact. She didn't just enter her profession, she thrives in it with compassion, confidence, and calling.

In her own words:

"My success is rooted in Christine's support, her belief in me, and her ability to call out who I am becoming. She nurtured my vision, strengthened my character, and helped me build a life aligned with purpose. I'm not just working in my field today—I am thriving in it. Christine doesn't build businesses or confidence alone; she builds legacy."

~ Dawn, Clinical Mental Health Counselor

Dawn's story is not about me.

It is about the power of identity, alignment, and becoming.

It is evidence that when a woman chooses to be the one, she creates room for others to rise—in their families, professions, and generations to come.

Every woman who chooses to lead boldly must first choose to live aligned. These are the same principles that helped me rise from survival to purpose, from hesitation to identity, and from silence to impact. They are not complicated—but they are deeply transformative when practiced with intention.

1. **Identity Before Strategy**

   Many women try to build results before they build themselves. But a strategy without identity leads to burnout, fear, comparison, and inconsistency. The first work is inward.

   - Ask yourself: Who am I becoming, not just what am I building?
   - Journaling prompt: What would I create if I fully trusted my calling?

- Inner practice: Speak your identity out loud daily.
- "I am called. I am equipped. I am trusted with purpose."

When you know who you are, decisions become easier, and opportunities become clearer.

2. **Abide Before You Strive**

Jesus taught that fruitfulness comes from abiding, not performing. When you're connected to purpose, you don't have to chase outcomes—you grow into them.

Practice spending ten minutes a day in silence before planning your goals.

- Ask: What is God inviting me to do, not just what the world demands I do?
- Reminder: Momentum comes from alignment, not pressure.

A rooted woman becomes a fruitful woman.

3. **Take Bold, Imperfect Action**

Your calling is strengthened when you choose to show up, even imperfectly. I wrote a book with no guarantee anyone would read it. I launched offers without applause. Courage builds clarity.

Show your commitment by writing one idea and deciding to pursue it for 90 days, no switching lanes.

- Replace perfection with obedience: Done is better than delayed.
- The goal is to create first, refine later.

Clarity is not the starting point; it is the reward for obeying the call.

4. **Build Before You Are Seen**

You don't become "The One" by waiting for recognition; you become it by becoming faithful in small beginnings. Your voice, your gifts, and your message must be developed before they can be amplified.

What you focus on grows, so focus on serving the one person who needs what you carry today.

- Ask: Who can I help now with what I already know?
- Practice creating value weekly—even when no one is watching.

Results do not prove your purpose. Faithfulness does.

5. **Lead With Lift**
   A woman called for more is not called only to rise—she is called to lift. Leadership is not just about achievement; it's about the impact that helps others walk into their own assignment.
   Mindset shift: "My success is a seed, not a trophy."
   - Ask: How does my growth nourish others?
   - Practical Exercise: Identify three ways your gifts help others flourish (not just be inspired)

   When your purpose includes others, God expands your influence.

Ready for the Next Step?

Download the *You Were Made for More Clarity Guide: Simple Practices for Alignment, Purpose, and Tangible Transformation* at ChristineNaluzze.com.

Christine Naluzze is the catalyst whom leaders and purpose-driven individuals turn to when they're ready to rise into their next level but feel blocked, unclear, or out of alignment. Known as the "Transformational Bestie," she blends faith-based wisdom with practical, soul-centered strategies that help people break limiting beliefs, reclaim their God-given identity, and activate lasting transformation in spirit, soul, and body.

For over two decades, Christine has guided women, professionals, nonprofits, and corporate teams from overwhelm to clarity and from stagnation to purpose-driven momentum. As founder of **Made for More**, she leads a thriving movement of women committed to living fully and leading boldly.

Her signature message—that every person is gifted, essential, and created for impact—shows leaders how to ignite productivity, deepen cohesion, and build cultures rooted in trust and purpose. Christine's work leaves every audience with this reminder:

You are made for more—and the power to rise is already within.

Get instant access to "**You Were Made for More Clarity Guide: Simple Practices for Alignment, Purpose, and Transformation**." A reflection guide to help you reconnect with your identity, align with purpose, and create meaningful momentum in your life.

ChristineNaluzze.com

Christine@ChristineNaluzze.com

Chapter 3

Stepping From 'Impossible' Into 'I'm Possible': Being The One For Myself Who Attracts Lasting Love

Barbara Magro Berg

Attract Your Soulmate Mentor

Stepping From 'Impossible' Into 'I'm Possible'

For many years, I built fabulous business partnerships working with corporate clients from New York to Hawaii, Florida to the Caribbean, and California to Australia... yet I couldn't build the one relationship that mattered most to my heart and be the one I needed for myself, in my own life. That contradiction became the defining catalyst of my life—and an invitation to look deeper.

My career in travel advertising sales wasn't just a job—it was the realization of a lifelong dream born the moment I fell in love with travel as a child. For over four decades, I lived and breathed the luxury travel publishing world, representing iconic brands like Condé Nast Traveler, Bride's, Australian Gourmet Traveler, Gourmet, and Luxury Travel Advisor magazines. My work carried me across continents and oceans, introducing me to remarkable people in food, travel, and tourism. I shared powerful conversations with visionary marketing leaders, transforming stories and strategy into business partnerships that brought travelers' dreams to life.

I also learned a profound truth that resonated deeply within me: tourism only thrives where peace exists. You'll never see travel ads for nations at war—yet places like Japan and Vietnam, once battlegrounds, are now on top of global travel lists. I watched tourism reshape lives, lift communities, expand career opportunities for youth, break down barriers, and open hearts through cultural understanding.

My career aligned with my values. In business, I was the woman who could make things happen—polished, respected, and at the top of my game with my passport as my constant companion.

But beneath my success lived a quiet ache—a longing for a deep, nourishing, intimate connection with the right life partner. Someone with mutual values, compatible dreams who would walk beside me, sharing laughter, and the life I had worked so hard to build—a man who would truly see me, hold my heart gently, and never let it go. My soulmate...

Although I had mastered self-leadership in business, the very confidence that carried me through airports, trade shows, and client meetings vanished when it came to love. I could command any boardroom, navigate high-pressure negotiations with grace—but when it came to the tender terrain of my own heart, I felt fragile and uncertain.

I realized that to welcome the love I longed for, I first had to become the leader of my own heart and turn inwards—facing my fears, healing old wounds, opening my heart and mind to what had been closed, and becoming the woman ready to receive what she once only dreamed of.

Every skill I had honed in business would now be repurposed for the most personal project of my life: claiming my own heart and creating the love I had once believed was impossible. I had to learn how to "Be The One" for my own love life.

The Love that Remained Elusive

While my professional life thrived, my love life told a very different story. I met my first husband while traveling to the Great Barrier Reef–a long-held dream to learn to scuba dive that I gifted myself for my thirtieth birthday. He was my dive master: handsome, charming, and oh! that Australian accent! We began a whirlwind romance—exciting, magnetic, and all-consuming. Twenty-two years my senior and a retired real estate broker turned scuba diver instructor, our romance felt like destiny. But beneath the exhilaration lay fundamental differences I ignored during the exciting intoxication of new love. We married in Hawaii when I was 34, then moved to Australia. But, within the first year, our relationship crumbled, leaving my hopeful heart with pain so deep I didn't know how to soothe myself. I found myself alone, scared, and starting over in a foreign country where I had relocated to live with the one whom I had thought was my forever love.

Following those years, my emotional pain was real. I missed out on creating my own family and endured the loneliness of an unfulfilled longing. I wrestled with self-doubt about my ability to love and be loved, a feeling that seemed impossible to shake.

For nearly two decades, I dove into personal growth—reading multiple relationship books, attending spiritual and personal development workshops and classes. Although I was a great manifestor in other areas of my life, I kept repeating the same painful patterns in my love life—dating and meeting men who were unavailable with misaligned values. I secretly believed real love was impossible, and I kept attracting relationships that mirrored that belief.

I came from generations of stable, long, happy marriages on both sides of my family, yet lasting love seemed impossible and beyond my grasp–a paradox that both puzzled and frustrated me. It was the one place where everything I knew about manifesting for myself just seemed out of reach.

Transformation and Attracting My Soulmate

After decades of suffering in my love life, something in me finally rose up and whispered, "*No more.*" A deeper resolve took root, and with the support of a relationship mentor, I discovered the profound power of the thoughts that triggered my beliefs and began applying the same scientific principles of manifestation that had always guided my professional success. After being divorced for almost twenty years, I shifted from searching for the right partner to *becoming* the woman whose heart, mind, and energy were aligned with the love she longed for. I realized love was about evolving into a new version of myself–one capable of receiving the aligned partnership I had dreamed about.

With courage, I began to face the old beliefs that had quietly shaped my thoughts for years: *I'm too old... It's too late... I'm too much...* Something must be wrong with me... It's impossible. One by one, I dismantled these old stories and replaced them with truths rooted in clarity, self-worth, and deservingness. My thoughts, words, and feelings became intentional acts of creation. I practiced daily alignment: visualization, journaling, gratitude, and EFT (Emotional Freedom Technique™) tapping to release blockages and replace them with a deeper truth...

I was not born to be alone.
I was born to love and be loved.
Love is my Divine Right.

I committed daily to my own self-love and raising my emotional vibration. In essence, I became "The One" for myself first.

I stopped my self-sabotaging thoughts. I learned I never had to chase true love—instead, by removing the barriers within that had prevented its arrival, I could magnetize it to me with ease. This was a very different energy than what I used in business *to make things happen*! I began to relax about it, imagining it already existed by visualizing and "feelingizing" a partnership that was joyful, nourishing, and aligned with my values. I also set my intention that it would naturally find me. Each day, I grew a little more into the woman who knew—deep in her heart and soul—that soulmate love was no longer impossible. It was already on its way. Slowly and unmistakably, my energy began to shift.

And, in a way that only the magic of the Universe could orchestrate, the most unexpected thing happened: in August 2016, Kevin found me. He embodied every quality that mattered to my soul. Our connection was effortless, grounded, aligned, and full of joy—the kind of love that doesn't need to be forced, explained, or justified. I experienced firsthand the transformative power of conscious creation, clarity, and aligning one's heart and mind for love.

Up to this point, the cost of not healing my negative patterns in love was steep. It cost me the possibility of being a mother and the joy of raising my own family. That loss lived in my heart for a long time.

But Kevin opened another door that my old beliefs thought was closed forever. Through him, I experienced a new kind of family and a dimension of love I never imagined would unfold. He came with two grown married children and three young grandchildren. And since our union, we have been blessed with four more little ones, bringing our total to seven! Their presence fills a quiet ache I had carried for decades, as if life whispered, "*You didn't miss out—you just received your vision differently.*" I am profoundly grateful.

This is the Magic of Soulmate Love—living proof of the manifesting principles that shift "impossible" into "I'm possible."

Being The One for Yourself: Shifting from Impossible to I'm Possible

What I once thought impossible, I now live as "I'm Possible"—having attracted my soulmate and the family I once believed I'd missed. My story is proof of the power of resilience, reinvention, and self-leadership at any age.

This experience inspired my "4-Step Scientific Love Formula," blending neuroscience, spiritual rituals, and practical tools I created to help ambitious women release old patterns, build confidence, and magnetize lasting, aligned love.

Meet my client Camilla, a successful Miami construction company owner in her late forties, single and never married. Despite her achievements, she felt unseen in love, tolerated relationships that didn't honor her, carried old wounds that made vulnerability feel unsafe, and felt trapped in repetitive patterns. But she reached a point where she was ready to break them and choose herself.

She contacted me last summer and said, "I'm ready to attract my soulmate."

Through my program, Camilla realized that aligned love wasn't something she had to chase—it was something she could attract once she gained clarity and stepped into her own self-worth. She took the powerful leadership skills that she used every day at work and turned them inward, becoming "The One" for herself first—honoring her desires, needs, and her boundaries.

For her, that meant moving out of the home she shared with her mother and aunt and releasing the pressure of always being the caretaker. She practiced energetic healing with EFT, repaired old wounds with her father, softened her energy, and opened her heart.

And then it happened.

This past spring, she met her soulmate. Within three months, they joyfully committed. She now says, "I never imagined love could feel this easy."

Consider Tasha, an ambitious, wealth mentor and divorced single mother, who was unaware of the blind spots blocking her from attracting a high-quality, aligned partner. Despite her career success, she kept repeating patterns in love, attracting unavailable men who didn't measure up to the woman she had become.

She began my program in December and was fully engaged in everything I teach. She set an intention to meet her soulmate within 120 days, and on day 121, she went on her first date with the man she married, and they recently celebrated their third anniversary.

Tasha says, "I encourage you to commit fully to the program like I did because if your heart is longing for the kind of love that would blow your mind, this program will help you have that."

The transformation of these two ambitious women shows what becomes possible when a woman becomes "The One" for herself first.

Coaching Philosophy and Signature Program

Inspired by the scientific principles of manifestation, I implemented them in my own life. While studying Wallace D. Wattles' *The Science of Getting Rich*, I created my own signature program that guides women on a structured journey from longing to lasting love—no matter what your age or history.

At the core of my work is my book, *The Science of Attracting Your Soulmate—4 Steps to Love & Happiness with Ease.* I don't offer quick dating tips; instead, I teach the scientific principles of manifesting, share spiritual practices and practical tools to release any old limiting beliefs, and provide a clear framework that guides women through a transformation process. Through aligning their mindset, emotions, and energy, they become magnetic to receiving the love they desire—the same steps I used to attract my soulmate, Kevin.

Through online workshops, private mentoring, group programs, as well as live immersive retreats in the Green Mountains of Southern Vermont, I guide women through this process with structure, accountability, and a soulful community. Becoming "The One"—confident, empowered, and open-hearted—isn't just an idea; it's a lived transformation that begins with clarity, intention, and courage for single women who are ready to take action and step into their new love story.

My guiding belief—"*Our thoughts create things, our words are our wings, and our feelings are the fire that makes our dreams come true*!"—reflects my philosophy that love is created from the inside out. Attracting a high-quality partner starts with purposeful thought, empowered self-respect, unwavering faith, a clear vision, and the ability to receive.

In this moment, you have a choice: stay stuck, believing love is "impossible," or step into your personal power and embrace "I'm possible."

Let me guide you on your love journey so that a year from now, your soulmate could be right by your side too!

I wish you deep, true, soul-recognizing love—the kind that starts from within and magically draws to you the right partner that recognizes the beauty of your heart and soul.

Barbara Magro Berg is a Loving Relationship Coach, author, speaker, and former global advertising sales executive who empowers single professional women to overcome inner barriers and attract lasting love.

Before becoming a transformational guide, Barbara built an extraordinary career at the forefront of luxury travel media as a top-tier sales leader representing the world's most respected travel and lifestyle magazines, including *Condé Nast Traveler, Gourmet, Bride's*, and *Australian Gourmet Traveler*.

Yet despite her accomplishments, Barbara's personal life told a very different story. After a heartbreaking divorce from her Australian husband at age 34, she spent nearly 20 years repeating painful patterns with unavailable men. Through deep inner work, spiritual practices, and an unshakeable commitment to growth, she attracted her soulmate, Kevin, who is now her husband. Today, she embraces the joy of being a stepmother and step-grandmother, gifts she once thought she would never experience.

Drawing on her own transformative journey—from heartbreak to "Big Love"—Barbara developed her "4-Step Scientific Love Formula," blending neuroscience, spirituality, and Emotional Freedom Technique (EFT) to help women align mindset, emotion, and energy. She is the author and creator of **The Science of Attracting Your Soulmate** (available on Amazon).

Take the first step on your love journey, uncover the hidden patterns keeping love at bay, and discover how ready you are to receive the deep, aligned relationship you've been longing for by taking her free **Attract Your Soulmate Quiz**.

Go to ▶ TheScienceofAttractingYourSoulmate.com/Quiz

TheScienceofAttractingYourSoulmate.com

Barbara@TheScienceofAttractingYourSoulmate.com

Chapter 4

The Thread That Pulled Me Here

Mary Jane ("MJ") Charles

Award-Winning Author | Speaker | Founder, The Caregiving Consortium

The Thread that Pulled Me Here

It began, unexpectedly, in a Zoom room with forty other entrepreneurs. We were asked to share the origins of our work—what planted the seed, and what kept it alive. One after another, people spoke with honesty and vulnerability. Many were caregivers of one kind or another: nurses teaching self-care, holistic practitioners restoring balance, therapists guiding people back to themselves, and several of us who mused over having the same calling but not having a certificate in any particular nursing skill.

As I listened, something inside bothered me. I wouldn't call it "competitive." Why would I compete with a nurse? I felt their feelings. I understood their words. Though I speak in my own words, I dared to think they would understand me as well. It was a tribal dialect. When my turn came, I surprised myself with what came out: "I'm a caregiver too!"

The Fog of Schizophrenia

My caregiving began early and quietly, long before I thought of it as "a job." There was PopPop, my Irish grandfather, who lived with us until he died at ninety-three. I was six, slipping his socks on in the mornings, laughing with him about the leprechaun who stole the missing sock. It would be OK with me if he took a nap in the middle of a card game. This was patience in action, and the gentle steadiness of simply being with someone when they can no longer get around.

My family's sense of care was evident as time went on. It was through observation that I learned firsthand how a tragedy can connect people, rather than tear them apart. Though much younger, I felt as important as anyone else in the room. In my late teens, I processed the fact that my presence was a well-intentioned distraction by the "Great Baby Planner" and not a "mistake," as a few would say teasingly. In fact, my parents needed me.

My presence was especially important in the 1960s. At home, my parents were confounded by a hush-hush topic at the time—mental illness. I was nine.

Bright, beautiful, and beguiling, my sister Judy fell into the fog of schizophrenia at the age of twenty. I watched my parents age as "the Judy problem" never left. Somehow, I had the wherewithal to step into a situation, conversation, or harrowing event and make a difference, adding some calm. My mother was brokenhearted, but she was tough. She would smile when I got home, but I knew she couldn't mask the sad song playing in her heart. I would put on one of my albums. She would tilt her head as if to ask, "Are you nuts?" which, given the stress of the moment, would make all of us laugh! It's called presence—the quiet kind. The "protect-her-at-all-costs kind." The "hold-your-parents-together kind." We didn't call it caregiving. You just did it. I believe it was this preadult training that got me through what was coming down the pike.

The ALS

At twenty-two, I found myself caring for my husband. He had been diagnosed with ALS at the age of 22 in the middle of his senior year of college. This neuro-muscular disease is also known as "Lou Gehrig's disease". It remains incurable. Known for his athletic build (akin to a swimmer), his body grew weak, his voice faded, and frustration took the place of ease. These symptoms occurred in the first two years. Because his diaphragm and vocal muscles were rapidly deteriorating, we created our own way of communicating—hand signals, taps, and tiny gestures that worked... for a while. I was able to teach these to the daytime nurse and his sister, who was also a nurse. It was too frustrating for him to work with the rest of the family to learn the signals. A type of familial atrophy was taking place at the same time in his body.

Days were spent in one room, as the rest of the family drifted around the edges of a house that never felt quite united. Professionals came and went. I worked full-time and came home to night care. A couple of church ladies took turns, arriving at 10 p.m. and staying until 6 a.m., when I woke up for the day. I slept in two-hour intervals, so I could roll him to avoid bedsores.

This routine lasted two and a half years. It was an epiphany that allowed me to make a decision that would change this path. I left.

Not in anger, not in guilt. Rather, it was self-preservation, a concept I grasped much later. My mother understood. A lifetime family friend understood. My dearest friend encouraged me. My conscience was clear. I put my plan into action, again with the full encouragement and support of one particular "church lady." She gave me a big hug and told me, "You need to do this." I didn't go far. I simply left the environment.

I kept my job, so his insurance remained in place. He was medically well cared for by a full-time nurse with whom he had become very close. His sister, who was also a nurse, was also involved. This was one cause of the unrest—it was readily apparent I wasn't needed.

My Time for Understanding

When I look back, I see that leaving saved me. I never returned, nor was I invited. He died six months later. I returned to college a few years later. I found it cathartic to write papers based on everything that happened during those five and a half years. I applied my caregiving experiences to human resource topics. Everything from team building to dispute resolution was easily absorbed.

Upon completion, I realized my time spent on my studies was, in fact, eighteen months of therapy. I was able to write, explain, and talk about what went on. My stories were true, and how I used them in a constructive way to untangle what I had experienced just flowed.

My B.S. degree was my thirtieth birthday gift to myself. I was going to be OK. I was no longer living inside myself. It was OK to go outside again.

And go outside I did, not realizing how much all these early life experiences were preparing and shaping me to fulfill my purpose in supporting other caregivers to thrive as they survived the business of sickness and dying.

The Mini-Stroke

At the age of sixty, I found myself driving my seventy-one-year-old husband to a long overdue meeting with his business partner. We never had a particularly close marriage. In this instance, he spent most of the prior year in California, building a home for his son.

It was finally completed. Time for him to come home. The car pulled into the driveway. He stepped out. One look at him and I immediately realized he was sick! He had lost a lot of weight; his clothes were baggy, his face was too lean, and his balance was uncertain. I waited for him to speak, but true to form, he said nothing.

More evidence that something was seriously wrong with him presented itself over the next few weeks. I discovered he could no longer button a shirt or tie his shoes properly. Even shaving his face was hit-or-miss.

Confirmation that something was seriously amiss showed itself as we took down the Christmas tree. I wasn't strong enough to loosen the bolts holding the tree in place, so he got on the floor. After much straining, the bolts began to turn. I finished the process and stood up. He couldn't get up! We exchanged glances. "Mind your own business," was his retort. He was too weak to pretend. I started a log in which I would collect symptoms of all kinds, in case he went to the doctor.

Why not go to the doctor, you ask? Not a chance. He had some kind of childhood horror concerning his heart, and once old enough, he vowed never again see a doctor, and he didn't. Instead, he consulted "Dr. Google." I could only guess what he was worried about—maybe his heart? He talked about his back, but when asked to point to the spot, he pointed to his kidney area instead. Again, no call to the doctor was made. Yet, I kept notes over time, but I couldn't guess or share anything.

Then came the TIAs, transient ischemic attacks, or mini strokes.

It was late fall, complete with sleet and wind. A football game was on television. I was reading. It wasn't what he said, it was how he said it. I looked up to see his face sagging on one side. His eyes weren't working, almost in opposite directions. Somehow, I knew it was a stroke.

We lived in the countryside, so it took a few minutes for the ambulance to arrive. The 911 operator remained on the line with me. She could hear him in the background, scolding me for making such a call. This happened again a month later. Both times, the mini stroke was met with disdain and refusal to see a doctor. He signed the medical form presented by the EMTs regarding his refusal to go with them. He was his nasty self to the EMTs, all of whom I knew. (It was a very small town.) One EMT took me outside, explained what just happened, and apologized! I gave him a hug. It was a rough night for all.

There are six symptoms of a mini stroke. All you need to do is remember the acronym BEFAST and then call 911 immediately. BEFAST stands for: Balance, Eyes, Face, Arms, Speech, and Time. Time is of the essence. His obvious fear of not knowing what was wrong, as well as the loss of control, were showing. His new routine of telling me how this was going to work was becoming more frequent and threatening.

While he was in California, I had complete peace at home. I remembered "me" before we were married. I wasn't afraid of him and his moods. In this moment, I held my ground. Low-voiced and steady. I simply stated that my calling EMTs is a basic call one human makes for another. I would make two more calls in the next few months, but I am no longer afraid. No, he never went to the hospital. He signed a "Refusal to Transport" each time. These events had a special place in my notebook.

I want to point out that I was not being unkind. There is just so much one can do for another person, even if they are "failing" right in front of you. It is their responsibility to want to help themselves. No one can do this for them.

The Medical Directive

I had been badgering him to get his final papers together. Though we had been married several years, I had no idea where his will was or if he even had one. I knew he didn't have a medical directive. Forty years earlier, when I cared for the ALS patient, there was no such thing as a medical directive. I lived through the havoc wrought due to the absence of any patient direction at that time. Now, a medical directive is legally required in many states before medical decisions can be made. He was of the belief that this wouldn't happen to him

He was deteriorating a little more each day. We were on the downside of this hill. On this day, he wanted to meet with his business partner. He was too exhausted to drive, so I agreed to take him. When we arrived twenty minutes later, I nudged him to let him know we were there. No response. I nudged again. No response. I looked directly at him. He wasn't sleeping. He had died in the car seat next to me.

As if by divine intervention, I asked him again about a medical directive before we left that morning. It occurred to me that perhaps he would allow me to read the state medical directive. (These are free online in most states.) I explained that I would read the questions in a "yes or no" fashion and use my phone's video, so there would be a record. He could nod or shake his head. He said yes! Fifteen minutes later, I had a video of his medical directive.

Not only did I have it, but the medical directive was also the first thing the ER doctor asked for upon my arrival at the hospital. The experience was surreal. I explained the events of that morning to the doctor, as I handed him my phone. He kindly responded, "This is Providence Hospital, after all.'

Other Important Documents

The meaning of caregiving can take surprising turns. This caregiving scenario took the cake, as it didn't end for another eighteen months. Though he was gone and the funeral was over, the estate remained in limbo. He never wrote a will. It was another year before it was closed due to the careless fact that there was no Will written. The estate was handled by the probate court of the state I lived in at the time. This meant the state made all decisions.

If he had any specific instructions, the state didn't care. He never wrote anything down.

This last devastating turn of events revealed the next turn in my path of caregiving. I became aware of all I had gathered in life by listening to others. I know this "stuff." I know how to get through it on the inside. I want to support other caregivers and help people prepare for the unexpected. Being prepared by knowing what to ask ahead of time removes fear in the moment as well as angst and unnecessary stress at a critically stressful time.

In May 2017, I published my first book, "Surviving the Business of Dying: Why Final Papers Matter." It was followed by a companion workbook, online classes, and working one-on-one to ensure that— in addition to a will—all the "little things" are taken care of in these matters ahead of time. My podcast, "**Caregiving for Caregivers,**" which brings professionals together to introduce themselves and answer questions, along with **The Caregiving Consortium**, is coming into focus.

Which brings me back to that Zoom room. Listening to others share their stories helped me see my own with new clarity. Caregiving isn't always medical. It isn't always recognized. It certainly isn't always paid. But the need to help runs deep. It binds those who care. And it deserves a place—a true gathering place of its own—where we can speak openly, learn from each other, and offer guidance in knowing they too will be OK after "the storm."

"And when the storm is over, you won't remember how you made it through, how you managed to survive. You won't even, in fact, be sure the storm is over. But one thing is certain. When you come out of the storm, you won't be the same person who went in."

~ Haruki Murakami

I am Mary Jane Charles, the creator and founder of **The Caregivers' Consortium**—a community where all caregivers, whether professional, familial, or the quiet helpers next door, can finally find their tribe. This is where the conversation truly begins.

Mary Jane ("MJ") Charles is the creator and founder of The Caregiving Consortium, a supportive community designed to unite caregivers of every kind—professional, familial, and everyday helpers who stepped in simply because they were needed. The Consortium offers a trusted space where caregivers can learn, share, and grow, and most importantly, know they are never alone.

MJ's path to this work began with her award-winning book, Surviving the Business of Dying: Why Final Papers Matter, honored as a 2019 International BookFest Finalist. Its companion workbook and monthly classes became the heartbeat of Last Wishes 'n Support, the home for her practical, compassionate instruction on gathering essential life details.

Her mission expanded through the Caregiving for Caregivers Podcast, where skilled practitioners and homegrown caregivers come together to discuss the realities and heart of caregiving, and through her monthly LinkedIn Newsletter, "The Caregiver's Compass," which provides ongoing tools and resources for caregivers.

Get your FREE checklist "**The Top 5 Actions You Can Take Today**" to support you in being prepared before the need arises.

Go to ▶ LastWishesNSupport.com

LastWishesNSupport.com

MJ@LastWishesNSupport.com

Section 2

Faith, Courage & Becoming

Once we begin to remember who we truly are, something powerful begins to shift.

Awareness alone, however, is only the first step. The next step asks something more of us. It asks us to trust the voice within and to act on it, even when the path ahead is uncertain.

Faith is often required before the evidence appears. Courage is required when the next step feels unfamiliar or uncomfortable. Yet it is in these moments that transformation begins to take shape.

The stories in this section reveal what happens when individuals choose to follow that inner prompting and take inspired action. They share moments of bold decisions, unexpected turns, and the resilience required to move forward even when the outcome is unknown.

Faith, Courage & Becoming is where potential turns into movement. It is where we begin stepping into the person we are capable of becoming and allow our lives to expand in ways we may not have imagined.

Chapter 5

Praying for the Impossible: Activating Mountain-Moving Faith

Pastor Dr. Dorothy Ross

Founder, Together We Rock Life, Inc.
Int'l Speaker, Author, CEO, Women Rocking Life

Praying for the Impossible: Activating Mountain-Moving Faith

"Ask, and it will be given to you; seek, and you will find; knock, and it will be opened to you."

~ Matthew 7:7

Every person of faith eventually faces something that seems beyond reach: Healing, Breakthrough, Restoration. A vision too big to make sense in nature. That's where this chapter begins with a story mission and the things you can't fix, but God can.

The Vision & Mission

My mission is to help people activate their faith to believe for the impossible through intentional, Scripture-rooted prayer. What inspires me is the countless number of people struggling with silent battles, health crises, financial strain, and emotional pain, yet still reaching for hope.

I believe God invites us to ask boldly, believe deeply, and receive expectantly. I am passionate about teaching believers not only to pray, but to pray effectively, knowing who they're praying to, what they're asking for, and how to align their words with Heaven.

This work is important to me because I've witnessed firsthand how a prayer grounded in God's Word can move mountains. The change I am in the world is to be a guide and encourager to those who believe against all odds.

Challenges & Lessons Learned

One of my most pivotal challenges came when my husband became ill and needed to go to rehab before coming home from the hospital. We hit an unexpected obstacle: we couldn't locate a birth certificate they needed, no official record to be found, no surviving family to confirm his details, and no clear path forward.

It didn't look good for us; my husband would have to come home instead of going to rehab. And if that happened, he would come home far too soon. I feared that without proper care, he might never recover and could become permanently bedridden.

It felt impossible. But instead of panicking, I applied the exact principles I teach. I wrote out the situation, listed the promises of God, found Scriptures, and prayed with gratitude, as if the breakthrough was already done. Around two-thirty in the afternoon, everything shifted.

Before I even finished my prayers, the phone rang. Two insurance agents, symbolically named Michael and Gabriel, had taken up the case. What had looked like a bureaucratic dead end turned into a breakthrough. My husband was approved and, on his way to rehab.

That experience taught me this: faith doesn't deny reality—it declares that God is greater than reality. That's the power of praying for the impossible.

Guidance, Strategies & Insight

Here are five key strategies that I use and teach to pray effectively:

1. **Know Who You're Praying To.** Choose one of God's covenant names that fits your situation: Jehovah Jireh (Provider), Jehovah Rapha (Healer), etc.
2. **Use the "6 W's Framework."** Who, What, Where, When, Why, and Which Scripture. This helps frame your faith clearly and intentionally.
3. **Two-Column Word List.** On one side, list challenges in one word. On the other side, list faith-based outcomes. Then find a matching Scripture for each positive word.
4. **Write Out Full Scriptures.** Don't paraphrase. Writing the full verse locks God's Word into your heart and mind.
5. **Start and End with Gratitude.** Begin every prayer with thanks as though the request is already done. End with a letter of gratitude to God. Faith is not passive. It's confidence in motion. The more you use it, the stronger it becomes.

Experiences, Case Studies & Examples

The story of my husband's hospital situation is just one of many I've seen transformed through intentional, faith-filled prayer. In workshops and mentoring sessions, I've watched people go from discouraged and defeated to empowered and equipped.

One woman who had been dealing with chronic illness for years began using the two- column exercise and started reading the verses out loud daily. Her mindset shifted, her faith increased, and her health began to improve, not just physically, but emotionally and spiritually. This work transforms people by giving them back their authority. It teaches them to speak God's Word over their lives, not with doubt, but with expectation.

Call to Action & Next Steps

If you're ready to begin your own journey of praying for the impossible, start with a sheet of paper and a Bible. Write your word list, find your Scriptures, and begin declaring them every day.

Want a head start? Download my free 7-Day Prayer Challenge and Faith in Motion at DorothyRoss.com/FaithInMotion.

To go deeper, you can connect with me on social media, join my prayer mentorship group, or bring these teachings into your community. My mission is to help you not just pray but receive it. Because with God, nothing is impossible.

The impossible is not a dead end. It's an invitation to pray boldly, believe deeply, and align with God's promises and not your problems. This is more than encouragement; it's a strategy—a way to pray effectively, scripturally, and expectantly.

Who Are You Praying To?

Before you start praying, ask: Who am I addressing?

We often hear names like Jehovah Jireh, which means "The Lord Will Provide." That name reveals God's nature in a specific situation—He provides. But it's important to understand that all these names are expressions of Jehovah, the covenant-keeping, self-existent God of Israel.

When you pray, know which attribute of God you're calling on:

- Jehovah Jireh – my Provider
- Jehovah Rapha – my Healer
- Jehovah Nissi – my Banner and Victory
- Jehovah Shalom – my Peace
- Jehovah Tsidkenu – my Righteousness
- Jehovah Shammah – the Lord is There

What to Pray – Using the "6 Ws" to Frame Your Faith

Use these six keys:

1. Who am I praying to?
2. What am I asking for?
3. Where is this affecting my life?
4. When do I need it?
5. Why do I believe it's possible?
6. Which Scripture supports it?

The Paper Exercise – From Problem, Process to Promise

Take one sheet of paper and divide it into two columns:

- Left Side: List, in one word, the problems you are facing
- Right Side: List a one-word promise or answer from God's Word. Find a Bible verse for each positive word. Write out the entire verse—word for word—and speak them aloud daily.

Problem	Promise
Fear	Courage
Worry	Peace

Joshua 1:9
"Have I not commanded you? Be strong and courageous. Do not be afraid; do not be discouraged, for the Lord your God will be with you wherever you go."

Thank God Before You Ask – and After You Believe

Gratitude is not just a response to answered prayer; it's the posture that positions you to receive.

Before you pray: "Thank You, God, that You already know my need and have already made a way."

After you pray: Write a thank-you letter to God in faith, as if it's already done.

How to Write Your Prayer (Template)

"Father, I come to You as [name of God – Jehovah Jireh, etc.]. Your Word says [insert verse].

I believe you are faithful to Your promises.

I ask You for [name your request] in full faith, knowing You hear me.

I receive it now, in Jesus' name. Amen."

Faith Declarations to Speak Every Day

- God hears me when I pray.
- I ask boldly and receive faithfully.
- My prayer is the key that unlocks Heaven's door.
- Even though I can't see it yet, I believe it's already mine.
- I don't beg for a breakthrough; I receive it by faith.
- My life is a testimony in the making.

Final Encouragement

You do not have to feel strong to pray strong. You do not have to have it all figured out to start. What you do need is to:

- Know Who you are praying to
- Know What He promised
- Know How to align your heart and words with His Word

Faith isn't pretending; it's standing on truth before it shows up in your reality. And when you pray the way God designed, intentionally, scripturally, and boldly—the impossible begins to shift.

Your mountain is already moving. Your miracle is already in motion. And your testimony is already written.

Pastor Dr. Dorothy Ross is a Golden Life Coach, international speaker, retreat host, and best-selling author devoted to empowering women to deepen their faith and discover the life-changing power of prayer. As the founder of Together We Rock Life, Inc. and CEO of Women Rocking Life, she mentors women around the world to invite God into every area of their lives and believe boldly in His promises.

With more than 25 years of leadership experience in corporate management and ministry, Dr. Ross combines practical wisdom with spiritual guidance to help women strengthen their faith, overcome life's challenges, and step confidently into their God-given purpose. Through mentoring programs, workshops, prayer groups, and speaking engagements, she inspires women to trust God fully and live with unwavering faith.

Dr. Ross is the recipient of several honors, including the Beacon of Hope Award for Christian Women Speakers, the Honorary Doctorate of Humanity Award, and the Lifetime Innovator Award from Women with Vision.

Her message is clear and powerful: with faith and prayer, women can step into a life of purpose by praying for the impossible.

Get started today with Pastor Dr. Dorothy. Want a head start? Download my free 7-Day Prayer Challenge and Faith in Motion.

Go to ▶ DorothyRoss.com/FaithInMotion

DorothyRoss.com & Porchtalklive.com

Info@DorothyRoss.com

Info.TogetherWeRockLife@gmail.com

Chapter 6

The Bold Approach to Your Life's Journey with a Plan to Survive & Thrive

Audrey Kirwin

The Preparedness Engineer

The Bold Approach to Your Life's Journey with a Plan to Survive & Thrive

This is a story of a life-changing pivot and the realization that all the skills, experiences, and challenges of my life have perfectly prepared me for this new direction. My current mission is to carry forward the legacy of the unfulfilled business dream of my dear friend Linda Fostek, who passed away in May 2023. I have been on a parallel career path of shared values, and her vision has always aligned synergistically with mine.

My prior career in the financial industry and my life's journey have repeatedly shown me that life provides lots of surprising situations, and it is critical to prepare for potential future events proactively. I have always been an entrepreneur and visionary. Linda and I had worked together as chapter leaders of the New York chapters of Women's Prosperity Network, educating women entrepreneurs on key concepts for building a business and making dreams come true. I remember when she first discovered her business path, and I had the pleasure of cheering her on during her journey.

Several unexpected life-changing events occurred in my life between 2021 and 2023. My dad had a stroke in November 2021 and became disabled. Then, the unexpected loss of my mom in March 2023, and eight weeks later, the loss of Linda. All of this, plus the ramifications of the COVID lockdowns, left my life in a tailspin. Linda's family was not interested in continuing her business, and I was too stressed to know what to do with it after she passed. I recognized that she had incredible ideas and vision. I could not let it die with her, so I rented a truck and moved everything into a storage unit.

The biggest challenge for me was deciding whether to stay on my current path or change direction. I passionately love the stock market and day trading. I have spent an extraordinary amount of time and money studying, practicing, visualizing, collaborating, and committing to the process of financial growth with extensive risk analysis and management. I resisted working on her business, and I did not want to do it exclusively. It became obvious to me that I could not successfully devote my time and energy to two primary directions. I needed to choose. I feared that I would regret passing up this business opportunity as I looked back on my life in old age.

After significant time and evaluation, I recognized the potential future impact that a new version of Linda's business could have on so many people. The turning point that propelled me forward in this new direction started with a phone call that led to an opportunity to solve a substantial problem in a vertical market. Over time, it led to the customer's commitment to move it forward as a pioneer of the new direction of *The Crisis Planners HOME System*.

The realization that my vision for this company is evolving has made me very passionate about sharing it with the world. Linda called herself "The Crisis Planner," and now I have created "The Crisis Planners," a team of people to carry out her legacy. The potential impact on families around the world who shift to a Preparedness Lifestyle would be extraordinary. Lives will be saved, financial stability can be maintained, and chaos and family battles can be significantly reduced or avoided. This shift to a proactive approach creates a feeling of empowerment and peace rather than fear and panic.

I have studied and shared Nancy Matthews' **The One Philosophy** for many years, and it has become part of the person that I am in every aspect of my life. My intended path as a day trader is truly my passion, but I am choosing to change direction to live my life boldly and be The One to carry Linda's message and dream forward. So many times, I felt I should do this, but I kept ignoring it. A series of things "coincidentally" happened, and thoughts of the possibilities unfolding in my mind were so fascinating, motivating, and compelling that I had no choice but to decide to commit to making a bold impact on the lives of families everywhere. I could feel the intensity of the energy inside me grow as I visualized this business's potential accomplishments. As many people have told me, the stock market will always be there, and I can revisit it in the future.

While planning for emergencies and major life events isn't new, most people still don't take action. Ignoring potential life events doesn't prevent them; it only leaves families unprepared.

This work matters because it shifts social norms from reacting to crisis to preparing for them. True preparedness is built through small, consistent habits practiced daily, rather than waiting until something goes wrong. Making this proactive shift can be life-altering for countless families and loved ones when a crisis occurs.

This business will build a community filled with like-minded people who love their families, want to protect them, and are willing to learn and invest in proactive planning. Emergency preparedness should be part of every person's life journey and provide a feeling of confidence and empowerment. It is impossible to stop pain, grief, disasters, illness, and problems. You can, however, prepare, rehearse, and give yourself and your family a better chance of a better outcome by being prepared rather than doing nothing.

Every time you take a trip on an airplane, the crew reviews the safety features and emergency protocols. You need to pay attention when they do this because if an emergency occurs, that's not the time you'll reach for the brochure located on the back of the seat in front of you to look for the instructions about where to find your floatation device or how to use it or why is the bag for the oxygen mask is not filling up to full size. It needs to be a familiar, automatic response.

The Crisis Planners HOME System is designed to create redundancies and a preparedness mindset to help you get ready for major life events. There are so many things that require attention that it can be overwhelming, often sending people into overload and analysis paralysis. The Crisis Planners Emergency Kits guide you through documenting and organizing all your important information redundantly using our trusted system.

Our solutions help you get:

- Documents organized and stored in multiple locations, including a secure cloud-based vault.
- Organized emergency lists of contacts, a summary of medical conditions, important documents relating to insurance, legal, financial, and other information to be part of an In Case of Emergency file that can be quickly accessed in both physical form and electronic version.

- A customizable Home Operations and Inventory Manual to document the details of your home, belongings, and operations of the household.
- Safety and Emergency Preparedness tools and ideas to proactively prepare for possible surprises.

These strategies take time to create and implement, and will only work if they are completed in advance. Our commitment is to make the process easier through a streamlined, guided system so that you actually do complete it.

Family chaos and fighting are horrible experiences after the passing of a family member and can be reduced or avoided. There are professionals in different industries, whether attorneys, accountants, insurance professionals, or wealth advisors, who have been extensively trained to help people avoid the unexpected consequences after the passing of a family member. Everyone needs to plan for life events, whether expected or unexpected.

Linda wrote a book titled ***Shit Happens*** that guides people to create a "plan to survive and thrive when faced with life's personal and natural disasters," and her message is very compelling. Everyone has either read about these situations or experienced them, and proactive action can mitigate some of the turmoil.

As I look back over my life, it's clear that I have been steadily preparing to step up and take the lead with this business. My husband has a job that requires him to be away from home in every emergency situation and imminent storm. He always prepares for emergencies and is committed to making sure we are safe. I would be home with my son during very scary storms, and my husband would say to me, "We are ready, and you just need to know the plan and your action steps." He would buy things we might never use, and then he says, "Laugh at me and say it is ridiculous to purchase all these items, but when we need them, you won't be laughing, you'll be thanking me."

On September 11, 2001, terrible things happened in New York City. All mass transit stopped. Millions of people had to walk across bridges to get transportation and bus service to their homes. One preparedness lesson for my family and I is that we will never go anywhere without comfortable shoes. Being forced to walk miles through the city wearing the same shoes you put on that morning or walking barefoot—which many people did (especially women)—was very difficult. Always have comfortable shoes with you because you never know when you will be walking home.

Preparing for Natural Disasters

Hurricanes and other environmental disasters can sometimes have catastrophic outcomes. However, there are ways to mitigate the recovery process.

If you know a storm is coming and that you have supplies such as water, food, batteries, blankets, flashlights, and toilet paper to last for 30 days, as well as an evacuation plan with prepared backpacks, you probably will feel differently about the approaching storm. While there is still some fear of the unknown outcome, such as the storm's severity, there could be a calmer feeling knowing you have done all you could to survive it.

In contrast, many people experience fear and panic before a storm, especially when they need to shop for supplies—the store shelves are empty, or prices are much higher than usual. If you are ready for a storm and have created a plan and purchased supplies in advance, then you are prepared and will have fewer regrets about actions that you should have taken.

On October 29, 2012, Super Storm Sandy hit Long Island, New York, and most of our friends and family suffered. Homes, cars, streets, and businesses were flooded. Roads were blocked, and debris was everywhere. Most people were without power for more than four weeks, and it was frigidly cold. A friend and her family were trapped in the loft of their submerged home for two days with six feet of water contaminated by heating oil. That family lost everything and was not prepared. Gratefully, our home was spared, and we had most of my extended family staying over until the power returned. Everyone who stayed with us took advantage of all the emergency supplies that we had been accumulating.

Many went back to their home to protect them from looters. They were forced to live without electricity, heat, and other basic conditions that we take for granted every day. While my family was prepared, far too many of my neighbors and friends were not. And as a result, they suffered so much pain.

I read a story of a man who lives in California in an area prone to wildfires. He cleared the brush around his property and invested in a machine that pumped water from his swimming pool. He connected it to an unconventional sprinkler system that sprayed water onto his home and property. During the massive wildfires in January 2025, he was able to save his home by turning on the system and letting it run as he evacuated his family to safety. This man's life was changed forever by proactively planning and investing in something he might not have ever used.

Preparing for Personal Crisis Situations:

Have you ever experienced or known someone who has experienced what happens when a person dies without a will? The deceased's assets are all subject to a legal process called probate. This process is long, stressful, and expensive; all your personal information is public, and a stranger—a judge—decides how your money and assets are distributed. The outcome has nothing to do with your wishes, often not what your family would want either. This is not a desirable outcome, yet it constantly happens.

You've no doubt heard stories of many famous people who have passed away without proper planning. Some of them are Prince, Amy Winehouse, Sonny Bono, Howard Hughes, Aretha Franklin, Michael Jackson, John Denver, and Kurt Cobain. This process can cause disputes, lawsuits, fractures in family relationships, or the omission of family members by mistake. And the truth is, that it is avoidable pain. People need to regularly update their beneficiaries because, in some cases, former spouses receive money they do not deserve when beneficiaries are not kept up to date. There are attorneys who specialize in helping families proactively mitigate this foreseeable problem.

People hate to pay for life insurance; a few do not like to discuss it, but I have witnessed people who have lost a family member and suffered devastating outcomes. Grief and suffering are bad enough, but when you add long-term financial pain, it is a brutal reality. Widows are forced to sell their homes, uproot their families, or have no financial means to maintain their lifestyle. The best time to get good quality and affordable life insurance is when you are healthy and as young as possible.

You must proactively plan. You cannot fix problems after they happen; you can only prepare for them before they happen. In one second, your life can change forever, and you need to know what action steps to take.

I invite you to download a free copy of "And Now What? Life Planner and Survivors Checklist—What to do Before, Upon, and After the Death of a Parent, Spouse, or Loved One."

I challenge every reader who has people they love to take proactive action steps to keep their family safe and prepared. Discover *The Crisis Planners HOME System* and begin the journey of a proactive planning lifestyle.

Audrey Kirwin equips individuals, families, and organizations with tools, systems, and a mindset to prepare for life's most critical moments before they happen. Through her work with senior living communities, home-care providers, trusted advisors, and families nationwide, she helps reduce chaos, eliminate document confusion, and accelerate recovery when the unexpected occurs. Her message blends strategic foresight, real-life preparation, and compassionate leadership—empowering people to replace uncertainty with confidence and fear with readiness.

She is the CEO of The Crisis Planners LLC, which she relaunched in honor of her late friend and founder, Linda Fostek. Audrey has made it her mission to help families and organizations take control before, during, and after life's most difficult moments. With nearly 30 years in financial services since 1996, Audrey brings elite-level expertise in finance, insurance, leadership, entrepreneurship, and strategic planning. She was a consistent top producer in financial services, is a bestselling author, and a seasoned speaker who has addressed audiences of business owners, attorneys, accountants, and care-industry leaders nationwide.

Audrey lives in Port Jefferson, New York, with her husband, and is an avid sailor, skier, animal lover, market trader, and proud mom of an amazing son.

Preparedness is NOT LUCK, it is a PLAN. Contact The Crisis Planners today to schedule a complimentary strategy call and ensure you and your family are indeed prepared with a plan to survive and thrive.

Go to ▶ TheCrisisPlanners.com

✉ Audrey@TheCrisisPlanners.com

✉ TheCrisisPlanners@gmail.com

Chapter 7

From Shell to Sanctuary: The First Quad That Built Me

Robin Tasco

Powerhouse in a Hardhat
Certified & Master Electrician, Licensed Electrical Inspector, Electrical Plan Examiner, Author, Trainer, Speaker

From Shell to Sanctuary: The First Quad That Built Me

I have always believed that some lessons are taught, and others are inherited. My journey into real estate was both. Long before I ever laid a hand on a blueprint or submitted a permit application, I was learning—quietly, consistently—from the man who helped raise me. My stepdad was a master carpenter, the kind of craftsman who didn't just build structures; he built confidence. He built expectation. He built a belief system inside of me that said, "You can do this. You can build something extraordinary."

He used to tell me, almost casually, "Buy a multi-family dwelling. Let the property help you pay the mortgage." At the time, I did not understand the magnitude of that wisdom. I was young; I was listening, but I did not yet know that he was giving me the blueprint to financial freedom. What seemed like simple advice would later become one of the most powerful guiding principles of my life.

Finding My First Diamond

When the time came for my first home away from home, I was a newly married young mother looking for a place where my new life could take root. I didn't want just a roof—I wanted a foundation. A starter legacy. A place with enough structure to raise my family and enough potential to stretch into my future.

And then I found it: a single-standing quadruplex just four blocks from my childhood home. On paper, it was a "complete shell." In reality, it was a diamond buried deep beneath layers of neglect and abandonment. But to me? It was beautiful. It had possibility. It had purpose.

With acquisition funds and construction financing available, the timing was perfect. I remember calling my dad, excited like a little girl again, asking him to come see what I had found. The two of us walked through the property together—the worn floors, the sagging porch, the exposed framing. He inspected each space with the eye of a man who had transformed countless structures over the course of his lifetime.

The quad had three one-bedroom units on the ground floor. Two of them had enclosed porches that looked like they once held laughter and morning coffee. The third was smaller, without a porch, but it still had its own private entrance. I could already imagine tenants, families, and life happening in those spaces.

Our family unit was the crown jewel: a wide porch stretching across the front of the home and a matching deck on the second floor. Inside, the first floor held a large foyer and access to the basement. On the second floor, the master bedroom suite sat across from two additional bedrooms. And then there was the family room—sun-kissed, spacious, full of promise. Five rows of windows that my dad suggested to demo and replace with a pair of double French doors that will open onto the upper deck—and that's where my dad paused.

"You know what would make this perfect?" he said softly, pointing. "Wrap that deck around the back of the kitchen. Extend your living space. Make it flow."

It was a moment of pure creative harmony. My dad's vision met mine. A carpenter's touch layered onto a future builder's dream.

Building Upward and Outward

The third floor held even more potential, an open loft area, a bedroom, a bathroom, and a surprising amount of closet space. This level felt like a sanctuary, a place where my boys could grow, dream, and discover themselves. Every inch of this home felt like an invitation to build a life, piece by piece.

With my years of construction experience, stepping into the role of general contractor felt natural. I knew the process. I knew the pace. And I knew the responsibility. But even experienced builders need support. So, I brought on a construction consultant to help ensure every subcontractor's bid aligned with my construction loan.

This is the part people often overlook: the quiet diligence behind the scenes. The spreadsheets. The budget balancing. The contingency holdbacks. The "measure twice, cut once" mindset, not just in carpentry but in financial planning.

I designed the layout for each apartment, every wall placement, each outlet location, the flow from room to room. With the help of an architect, I refined the plans and then submitted everything to the City's Licenses & Inspections office.

That's when the first big surprise landed in my lap.

Zoned for More Than I Expected

Before I could pull permits, I was told something that stopped me mid-stride: the property wasn't zoned for four units, it was zoned for five.

Five?
I had prepared for four.
My plans showed four.
My budget was based on four.

I now had two choices:
Resubmit my plans for a five-unit building
OR
Proceed with four and forfeit the ability to convert back to five later.

It was a defining moment because so much of real estate investing is decision-making under pressure. Choosing clarity over complexity. Choosing flow over frustration. Choosing what your life can handle, not just what your ambition wants.

I chose four.
I chose simplicity.
I chose what aligned with my vision, my family, and my future.

The Break That Reshaped the Build

Once I overcame the zoning hurdle, everything seemed back on track. Quotes came in for plumbing, heating, and drywall. I prepared to handle all the electrical work myself. And I waited—patiently—for just one more estimate: my dad's carpentry numbers.

But life is not linear. Even the strongest relationships face storms.

My father and I had a falling out. A deep, personal break that shook me emotionally and structurally. Suddenly, the man I counted on—the craftsman whose touch shaped so much of the home—was no longer part of the project.

And that changed everything.

Finishing carpentry is not like any other trade. It's intimate. It's precise. It's the difference between "okay" and "art." Drywallers can close a wall and can spackle a smooth seam. But a finishing carpenter is the one who defines the home's personality—doorways that close clean, trim that hugs the corners, moldings that elevate the room.

And without my dad, I was left to find someone else who could rise to the level of quality I expected.

I vetted carpenters like my life depended on it: interviews, walkthroughs, references, trial tasks. Some were decent. Some were questionable. Some talked a better game than they played.

But none were my dad.

None had his eye.

None had his legacy in their hands.

And in that struggle, a new lesson was born.

Experience: The Greatest Vetting Tool You'll Ever Have

As investors, we love numbers. Bids. Comparisons. Estimates. But here's the truth: You don't know a contractor until you work with them.

You can collect two, five, or even ten bids. You can analyze every detail, every material cost, every timeline. And still, none of it replaces the truth that only emerges once the work begins.

Relationships in real estate aren't built in interviews.

They're built in sawdust.

They're built in communication.

They're built in showing up—day after day, project after project.

That experience taught me to start small.

To start manageable.

To partner with people who grow with you, not just bid for you.

Because the real vetting tool?

The one that never lies?

The one that shapes your future as an investor?

It's the work.

It's the real boots-on-the-ground, in-the-field experience that tells you who's consistent, who's committed, and who you can trust.

And I stand by that advice—unapologetically.

Build With Intention

Your first property will shape you as much as you shape it. Whether you're standing in front of a diamond in the rough or dreaming of your first investment, now is the time to move from inspiration to action.

1. **Start With a Property You Can Grow Through**
   Choose a project that stretches you but does not break you. Begin with a size, scope, and budget you can realistically manage while learning the ropes.
2. **Build Your Team Before You Need Them**
   Don't wait until you're in crisis to find your carpenter, plumber, electrician, architect, or consultant. Start forming relationships now—quality partners are built over time, not in emergencies.
3. **Walk Every Property Twice**
   The first walkthrough is for excitement.
   The second is for reality.
   Take notes. Take pictures. Take your time.

4. **Learn the Power of Permits, Zoning, and Compliance**
   Don't assume—verify. Understanding zoning and permitting early prevents costly surprises later.
5. **Vet Contractors Through Real Work—Not Just Estimates**
   Collect bids, yes, but pay attention to communication, professionalism, punctuality, and willingness to walk the job with you. True vetting happens on-site.
6. **Honor Your Vision and Adapt with Grace**
   You will face delays, disappointments, and unexpected turns. Stay flexible, but don't lose the heart of your vision. Build with intention, not impulse.
7. **Commit to Learning as You Build**
   Every project teaches a lesson. Document what worked, what didn't, and what you'll do differently next time. Your experience becomes your greatest asset.

Reflection Questions: What Is This Project Building in You?

1. What early messages or memories shaped how you think about home, building, or ownership?
2. What is the "diamond in the rough" you feel drawn to right now—in real estate or in your life? Why does it speak to you?
3. When have you ignored your own instincts on a project or decision? How would things have changed if you had trusted yourself?
4. What kind of property or project feels manageable for you to start with? What excites you about it? What intimidates you?
5. Who are the people you want on your future team—contractors, mentors, partners? What steps will you take to begin building those relationships now?
6. Where in your life do you need to choose clarity over complexity? What decisions can you simplify?

7. How do you respond when someone you were counting on steps away or disappoints you? What strength did that moment reveal?
8. What skill, habit, or mindset do you need to grow into before you take on your next investment or renovation project?
9. What does "building with intention" mean to you personally?
10. How will you document your journey so your future self—and others—can learn from it?

The Home That Built My Voice

Looking back, that first quadruplex wasn't just a project—it was a teacher. It taught me to trust my instincts. It taught me resilience. It taught me to pivot gracefully. It taught me that even when people step away, your purpose does not.

That building strengthened my voice, sharpened my skills, and prepared me to teach others. It became the blueprint for the lessons I now share with new investors, future homeowners, women entering trades, and anyone brave enough to build something from nothing.

Every broken beam I replaced, every new wall I framed, every decision I made under pressure, it all built me, long before I became the mentor, the educator, the real estate inspector, and the investor I am today.

This wasn't just my first property.
It was my first becoming.

And to this day, I stand firm on this truth:

There is power in what you build, but even more power in what building teaches you about yourself.

Robin Tasco is a powerhouse in a hardhat, a certified and master electrical inspector, licensed electrical inspector, electrical plan examiner, and fearless pioneer in the construction trades. With more than 30 years of expertise, she became the first female union representative for IBEW Local Union 98 and the Philadelphia Building Trades, breaking barriers with courage, integrity, and undeniable skill. Her leadership has opened doors for women and people of color in non-traditional industries.

A sought-after speaker, trainer, and author, Robin speaks from the heart on inclusion versus true belonging. She is the founder of Tasco Solutions and Tasco Contractors, author of "Can You See Me Now," and bestselling co-author of "How to Break the Glass Ceiling and Keep It Nice."

Robin infuses her work with spiritual insight, drawing strength from the wisdom of Florence Scovel Shinn and the belief that we are all magnets creating our own reality. Her unwavering truth-the message woven into her life, her leadership, and her legacy is simple and powerful: "***I am magnificent, no matter what.***"

Get your copy of Robin's free ebook "You Are Not Alone" as well as her "7-Point Property Checklist Every Real Estate Investor Needs."

RobinTasco.com

Robin@RobinTasco.com

Chapter 8

It's Never Too Late to Rejuvenate

Beverly Brooke Peterson

Lady Rejuvenator

It's Never Too Late to Rejuvenate

Today, like so many mornings before, I began with a simple prayer:

"Let me BE THE ONE for someone today."

That prayer has guided me through countless challenges, divine coincidences, and moments of awakening. I've learned that when you sincerely ask to be of service, life rearranges itself to answer.

A Divine Nudge at Huckleberry's

One afternoon, I felt a strong inner nudge to stop at a little Southern restaurant called Huckleberry's. Nothing remarkable about the place at first glance, but I've learned that intuition often whispers through ordinary moments. When I sat down, I noticed a message printed on a waitress's T-shirt: "**Be my Huckleberry**."

Curious, I looked it up. The phrase means, "I'm the one for the job" or "I'm just the right person for a challenge."

The timing was too perfect. My spirit smiled. Once again, the universe was reminding me: *You are the ONE for the job.*

As I was finishing my meal, the waitress stopped to chat. She shared, through tears, that both her children were extremely ill and that doctors only offered more medications and little hope. She was exhausted and desperate to find "another way."

Right there at that moment, my prayer was answered. I was led to someone who needed encouragement, and she became my mirror—a reflection of why I continue to walk this path.

Being Lady Rejuvenator isn't a business title. It's a calling.

A Journey of Faith and Intuition

My story—like yours, perhaps—is an evolving one. It's a journey marked by faith, intuition, and a refusal to give up.

In 1999, I moved from California to Florida in search of a healthier, more holistic way of living. That move led me to the **Hippocrates Health Institute**, where I immersed myself in natural health and lifestyle transformation. For the first time, I felt aligned with my soul's purpose: helping others heal and believing in the body's innate intelligence.

But following intuition doesn't mean the path is smooth. In 2010, I faced one of my most painful professional challenges. I discovered unethical practices in the company I was involved with. My belief system crumbled overnight. I remember praying, "Help me, God. I don't know what to do."

And then—grace showed up.

I was introduced to **Women's Prosperity Network (WPN)**. The guidance, encouragement, and wisdom I found there rekindled my faith in humanity—and in myself. The three sisters who founded the organization, along with the extraordinary women who became colleagues and friends, reminded me how to honor myself, reclaim my confidence, and listen once again to my inner knowing.

That connection birthed my next chapter as **Lady Rejuvenator**—a title gifted to me by my WPN sisters.

When the Healer Must Heal Herself

For years, I focused on helping others find natural healing solutions while quietly facing my own battles. My husband was diagnosed with kidney disease and later, cancer. Together, we chose an alternative path. With faith and natural methods, he lived another fourteen meaningful years.

During that time, I learned one of life's great lessons:

Healing is not only about the body—it's about spirit, connection, and courage.

After COVID, in 2021, I was diagnosed with COPD (Chronic Obstructive Pulmonary Disease). Managing my declining health while supporting my husband's needs became overwhelming. Despite exploring every promising supplement and holistic product, nothing truly reversed my lung damage. My faith wavered, but my intuition kept whispering: There's another way.

When my husband passed in August of 2021, I found myself at another crossroads—grieving, exhausted, and uncertain. Then, life surprised me again.

A friend convinced me to try a senior dating app, and the first person I connected with turned out to be a neighbor I had from forty-five years earlier! That reunion blossomed into a beautiful friendship and companionship—proof that even after loss, love can find you again.

Still, my health continued to decline. I developed recurrent infections and breathing difficulties. By 2023, I was diagnosed with Acute Respiratory Failure, spending five days in the ICU and three weeks in rehabilitation. 2024 was a challenging time for me.

That year contained many revelations! Mostly, that I was unable to care for myself, and I needed to move in with my daughter and son-in-law, who had lovingly built a mother-in-law suite for me—a divine preparation I hadn't foreseen.

But the truth is, I nearly gave up. The endless medications, side effects, and continuing lung infections left me depleted. At one point, six lung infections in four months pushed me to the edge. I cried out in prayer, "G*od, either take me now or show me another way*."

When the Student Becomes the Miracle

The very next day, my naturopathic doctor called about a new company offering advanced natural products. Skeptical but hopeful, I listened. To my amazement, one of my old colleagues from Florida was part of that company—and she shared photos and results that defied everything I'd been told about "irreversible damage."

I decided to try the products. Within two days, I began coughing up hardened mucus that had restricted my breathing for years. Soon after, I no longer needed my daily oxygen devices.

Tears streamed down my face as I realized—I was witnessing my own rejuvenation. My body wasn't done healing. My mission wasn't over.

That experience reignited my passion and affirmed my divine assignment: to BE THE ONE who proves that **it is never too late to rejuvenate**—in body, mind, or spirit.

Rebirth of Lady Rejuvenator

Today, at 83 years young, I continue to walk the path of healing and purpose. My body may have faced countless battles, but my spirit is stronger than ever. I am here not merely to survive, but to inspire others to trust that spark of intuition that whispers, "*Try again.*"

When I ask, "Who am I? Why am I here?" the answer rises clearly within me:

You are Lady Rejuvenator. You chose this path to remind others that renewal is always possible.

I now dedicate my energy to supporting others in the Natural Healing Product community, helping them remember that their bodies are intelligent, their spirits are resilient, and that healing is not only reserved for the young.

If I can heal, so can you.

Lessons from the Journey

Every step of this journey has taught me something vital about life, intuition, and the power of persistence. Here are a few lessons I've gathered along the way—wisdom you can apply to your own path of rejuvenation:

1. **Listen to Your Inner Whisper**
   Your intuition is your divine GPS. It may not shout; it may only nudge—but it is always guiding you toward alignment. When I felt drawn to *Huckleberry's*, it wasn't about getting food. It was about meeting someone whose pain mirrored my purpose.

Take time to get quiet. Breathe. Ask your inner wisdom, "What is my next right step?" Then trust the answer—even if it doesn't make logical sense at first.

2. **Follow the Breadcrumbs of Synchronicity**
   Life constantly offers hints—people, signs, or phrases like "Be my Huckleberry." The more you acknowledge these synchronicities, the stronger they become. Coincidences are confirmations that you're on the right track.
3. **Don't Let Age Define Your Possibility**
   Too many people believe their best days are behind them. I'm living proof that purpose doesn't retire. The body can regenerate. The heart can reopen. The spirit can reignite at any age. Healing and transformation are timeless.
4. **Embrace Communities of Light**
   Isolation feeds despair. When I joined Women's Prosperity Network, I discovered that surrounding yourself with people who believe in your brilliance is a form of medicine. Seek communities that remind you of your strength when you forget it.
5. **Turn Pain into Purpose**
   The health challenges that once made me question my worth and purpose became the foundation of my calling. Each obstacle prepared me to guide others through theirs. Whatever tugs at your heart most deeply points toward your highest service.
6. **Keep Asking for "Another Way"**
   When the world says, "There's no hope," keep asking. Ask your Creator, ask your intuition, ask your higher self. The moment you ask sincerely, the answer begins to unfold. Healing may not arrive in the package you expect, but it will guide you like a Guardian Angel!
7. **Choose to BE THE ONE**
   Being The One isn't about perfection; it's about presence. It's about saying, "*I'm willing to be the one who believes, the one who tries, the one who shows what's possible.*" You never know whose life you'll change simply by living your truth.

A Call to Rejuvenate

To everyone reading this, I want you to hear this truth in your bones:

It is never too late to rejuvenate.

You may feel tired, discouraged, or disconnected. But inside you are the sparks that cannot be extinguished. The sparks are your divine blueprint—they remember who you truly are.

- Take one small step today to honor your body.
- Breathe deeply.
- Drink water with intention.
- Step outside and let sunlight kiss your skin.
- Speak kindly to yourself, forgive people and issues.

These simple acts awaken your cells and your soul.

When you do, you become the living embodiment of renewal. You become The One who inspires others to believe again.

Closing Reflection

As I continue this journey, I know my purpose more clearly than ever. I am here to remind others—especially those who think it's too late—that rejuvenation begins the moment you decide to believe again.

I am Lady Rejuvenator.

I am still breathing, still learning, still healing, and still shining.

And so can you.

Because it's never too late to rejuvenate—and it's never too late to BE THE ONE.

Beverly Brooke Peterson, affectionately known as the Lady Rejuvenator, is living proof that aging can be vibrant, joyful, and full of purpose. At 83, she helps seniors reclaim their energy and vitality through the healing power of food, mindset, and modern natural modalities.

A graduate of the Hippocrates Institute and a certified Raw Food Chef and Health Educator, Beverly has dedicated her life to uncovering treatments that restore the body's original, self-healing design.

She stays on the cutting edge of new recipes, plant-based remedies, and innovative delivery systems—including products that fuse nature's molecular wisdom with today's most effective healing technologies.

Before her wellness mission, Beverly was a top-tier headhunter in Silicon Valley for 25 years, known for her uncanny ability to match the right person to the right opportunity. Her deep intuition, resourcefulness, and people-reading gifts continue to set her apart in the healing world today.

Her mantra: "Let your food be your medicine, and your medicine be your food." And she's here to show you—it's never too late to rejuvenate.

Get Instant Access to Lady Rejuvenator's guide on "How to Be a Victor at Any Age" using natural remedies, a resilient mindset and practical daily rituals that support your vitality and longevity.

Go to ▶ LadyRejuvenator.com

LadyRejuvenator.com

BeverlyBrooke@LadyRejuvenator.com

SECTION 3

Living & Leading As The One

Over time, something remarkable begins to happen.

The choices we make to listen, to trust, and to act on the whispers within begin to shape the way we move through the world. What once felt like isolated moments of courage gradually become a way of living.

Being The One becomes less about a single decision and more about a way of being.

In this section, the authors share what it looks like to embody the lessons learned along the way. Their stories reflect lives lived with greater awareness, compassion, alignment, and purpose. Leadership emerges naturally as they influence others not through authority, but through presence and example.

Living & Leading as The One is the ongoing expression of the journey. It is the realization that when we choose to live authentically and follow the deeper wisdom within, our lives can inspire others to do the same.

And that is how transformation begins to ripple outward into the world.

Chapter 9

Seeing The One

Dawn McCarter
Luminary Leadership Solutions

Seeing The One

Being The One doesn't begin with becoming the most capable, the most influential, or the most accomplished person in the room. It begins with how willing we are to truly see the person in front of us.

Long before anyone recognizes us as leaders, long before the awards or the titles or the credibility, we lead in small, unseen exchanges. The quiet moments where we choose to look into someone's eyes and meet them with truth, presence, and belief.

These are the moments that change trajectories.
These are the moments that shape cultures.
These are the moments that reveal who we really are.

I have long believed that every encounter holds the possibility of transformation. A grocery clerk. A coworker who seems withdrawn. A stranger whose forced smile hides a storm. Any one of them could be the person whose life bends because of what we offer. And if that is true, then we are invited into a way of living—and leading—that treats every person as "The One," not because of what they can do for us, but because of who they already are.

I was reminded of this truth on a single afternoon years ago, in a Sprint retail store tucked inside a busy district of my region. I was a director then, responsible for dozens of locations. It was an especially tense season for the team. Performance was lagging, pressure was high, and everyone felt the weight of expectations. By the time I arrived on site, the nervous energy was palpable. You could feel it in the air—the way associates straightened their posture when I walked in, the worried glances they exchanged, the manager trying hard to appear composed even as her eyes flickered with anxiety.

She was young, talented, and deeply capable. I didn't know her well, but in that moment, she was shrinking under the pressure. I could see that she feared I might criticize her, or worse. Maybe she feared for her job. Maybe she feared disappointing her leader, who wasn't there that day. Maybe she feared that this moment—this visit—would confirm her worst internal narrative.

I didn't need to know the details. I could already feel the truth beneath her fear.

So, I asked her quietly, "Can we step to the back for just a moment?"

Away from her team's eyes.
Away from the expectations of performance.
Away from the noise.

In the back room, with the door closed and the hum of the store fading behind us, her shoulders stiffened. She braced herself. I could see it—the armor of someone who has been holding too much for too long.

I didn't confront her metrics. I didn't ask about numbers or tasks or execution. I simply spoke to the person standing in front of me.

"I need you to hear something," I said gently. "You are wildly talented. You're doing so much more right than you realize. And the pressure you're carrying is dimming the very strength that makes you exceptional. You don't have to shrink here. You already are the leader your team needs."

Before I finished, the tears came—fast, unexpected, true.

She wasn't dramatic or loud. She simply broke open, as though someone had finally touched the truth she had been trying so hard to hide. Her posture softened; her breath returned. The tension uncoiled from her shoulders. And after that release came a steadiness, a quiet reclaiming of the leader she already was.

I gave her a moment. I looked down at my phone, quietly giving her the space to gather herself.

And then, without fanfare, she took a deep breath, wiped her eyes, and said softly, "Okay. I'm ready."

When we walked back out onto the sales floor, something in her had shifted. She stood taller. She spoke with clarity. When I coached the team through a few opportunities and asked for a quick role-play, she didn't shrink to the back or defer to me—she stepped forward. She chose presence. She led. And right there, in front of her team, she showed them not just who she could be, but who she already was.

Weeks later, at a regional meeting with hundreds of people milling around, she spotted me. She walked straight up, wrapped me in a hug that came from her soul, and said through tears, "It mattered, Dawn. It changed everything."

What changed things for her wasn't my title or authority. It wasn't a plan, a tactic, or a scorecard. It was being seen. It was the truth spoken in love. It was presence without judgment. It was someone treating her as "The One" at the exact moment she needed it most.

That is what leadership is.

Not the spotlight.
Not the strategy deck.
Not the endless striving to prove our worth or measure ourselves against someone else.

Leadership is the moment we choose to notice the person in front of us and offer the presence that lifts them back into themselves..

Over the years, I've taught leaders that three power skills fuel this way of being: truth, optimism, and presence.

They are not competencies on a résumé.
They are not trends.
They are not soft skills.

They are transformational skills—and they are accessible to every one of us.

Truth is love in action.
It is not harsh, punishing, or cold.
It is clean.
It is kind.
It is courageous.

Truth calls people higher—not through shame, but through recognition.

Truth says, "I see the strength you've forgotten."
Truth unlocks potential that pressure has buried.
Truth liberates.

Optimism is often misunderstood as naïveté or blind positivity. It is neither.
Optimism—real optimism—is fierce.

It is the willingness to see possibility even in the presence of challenge.
It is the belief that more is possible than the present moment suggests.
It is a choice to look for what could be instead of collapsing under what is.

Fierce optimism ignites people.

It makes them braver.
It invites them to imagine themselves in their next level.
It gives them permission to want more and believe more.

Presence is the quiet superpower of leadership.

Presence is more than proximity.
It is more than being in the room.
Presence is the radical act of humility that says:
"You matter enough for me to give you my full attention."

Presence listens to understand, not to prepare a reply.
Presence makes people feel safe.
Presence awakens dignity.

The truth is, presence changes everything.

Whether in a back room in a retail store, a boardroom, or a living room.

When truth, optimism, and presence converge, we begin to lead not from title, but from transformation. And from that place, every interaction becomes an invitation to elevate someone else.

Over the course of my career, I've watched extraordinary leaders make intentional choices like this again and again. The moments may look different, but the pattern is remarkably consistent.

These choices aren't complicated, but they are revolutionary when lived:

- They care deeply and act boldly, the Give a Damn factor.
- They choose kindness, not as a detour but as the path.
- They embrace and model resilience, understanding that resilience predicts success.
- They create and inspire joy because joy is not a perk—it is essential to a thriving life.
- They give themselves grace, knowing self-kindness sustains compassion.

These choices don't just shape results.

They shape cultures.
They shape families.
They shape futures.

Most of all, they shape how we make people feel.

And as Maya Angelou poignantly reminds us, people never forget how we made them feel.

The woman in that Sprint store didn't remember the exact words I said. She remembered how she felt in that moment—seen, believed in, and lifted. She remembered that someone treated her as "The One," and that single moment helped her reconnect with the truth of who she was.

And the truth is, I didn't just give that gift—I received the gift as well.

More than once, someone has looked at me with a clarity I didn't yet have, spoken a truth I needed, or offered a presence that steadied me. I remember those moments with such gratitude. They shaped me just as much as I shaped her.

That is the invitation of leadership.

Not to be the hero.
Not to be the savior.
Not even to be the expert.

But to be the one who sees.

The one who notices and speaks truth with compassion.
The one who believes fiercely and listens deeply.
The one who calls forth the greatness already present in others.

When we live this way, leadership becomes less about what we accomplish and more about who we elevate.

Less about performance and more about presence.

Less about being recognized and more about identifying the sacred worth of the person standing right in front of us.

Being The One is not about us.

It is about becoming the kind of person through whom transformation can flow—quietly, consistently, and with love.

And the most extraordinary thing?
When we treat every person as "The One,"
we quietly become the one our world needs.

Dawn McCarter is a leadership coach, speaker, and author who equips leaders to transform culture from the inside out.

If you want stronger leaders, healthier cultures, and a more human way of working, Dawn helps you create it through leadership rooted in clarity, courage, and compassion.

After nearly 25 years in executive leadership, she now teaches leaders to use kindness as both a strategic strength and a daily practice that transforms how we live, work, and connect. Her work blends lived experience, leadership insight, and spiritual depth to help people lead with purpose and presence.

As President of Luminary Leadership Solutions, Dawn offers executive coaching, transformative keynotes, and leadership development programs designed to create lasting growth. Through her partnership with Crestcom International, she also delivers curriculum-based leadership training that drives measurable impact inside organizations.

Her forthcoming book, *The Kindness Promise*, explores how the power and practice of kindness can enrich the human experience and transform how we live, lead, and connect.

Known for her empathy, fierce optimism, and steady presence, Dawn empowers leaders to elevate others and embody the impact they wish to create.

Dawn lives in Central Texas with her husband and has a deep love for animals, nature, sunsets, and the belief that kindness is one of the most powerful forces for good in the world.

Continue the journey with a free chapter from *The Kindness Promise*.

Go to ▶ DawnMcCarter.com/gift-chapter

DawnMcCarter.com

Dawn@DawnMcCarter.com

Chapter 10

Soul Medicine Arts: Remembering The Sacred Ways of Being The One

Dr. Diana Spirithawk, DSS

Soul Medicine Arts: Remembering The Sacred Ways of Being The One

I was not born into a family that honored spiritual experiences or spoke of Divine guidance. Yet from my earliest memories, I lived between two worlds—the waking world, filled with hardship and isolation, and the dream world, where I found comfort, connection, and a sense of belonging that waking life rarely offered.

Born with two debilitating conditions—a deformed hip and a cleft palate. I struggled to speak clearly and could not run or play like other children. So, I ran in my dreams. I sang, danced, flew, and escaped into realms where my spirit could move freely. As I grew older, dreams continued to meet me at turning points, offering comfort when the waking life felt too painful to bear.

Much of my childhood was spent alone, wandering in nature by day and traveling to magical places by night. I was not the "perfect daughter" my mother wanted. I became a lone wolf tossed by dysfunction, searching for love, and raising three children alone with little hope in sight. My only waking dream was a fantasy of studying with a Native American medicine man, something that seemed impossible for an uneducated single mother barely surviving.

Then a dear friend handed me "Black Elk Speaks." Its foreword promised that "if you read this book with an open heart, you will have a spiritual awakening." I longed for that. I prayed for that. And a few nights later, I received what I now recognize as my first "big" dream—a dream that awakened the destiny that had been whispering to me since childhood.

Throughout history, sacred texts recount how God speaks to us through dreams and visions. Moses, Joseph, and the prophets were all guided through the dream realm. Dreams remain God's timeless language, a bridge between heaven and earth, between who we are and who we are called to become.

My life transformed when I began honoring the messages of my dreams instead of dismissing them. What I now call **Soul Medicine Arts** emerged from this journey—six sacred practices for listening to Spirit, understanding divine messages, and embodying the wisdom revealed in dreams.

These are the arts that have guided my healing, shaped my purpose, and taught me what it means to Be The One—a vessel of Divine guidance and love.

The First Art: Listening for the Call of Spirit

Dreamwork begins with listening—not with the ears, but with the soul.

Spirit speaks through symbols, colors, emotions, metaphors, and synchronicities. To listen is to remember that you are never alone. The dream world is alive with guidance.

When I began keeping a dream journal and recording even the faintest fragments, a pattern emerged: a living dialogue between me, my soul, and the Divine. Dreams revealed where I resisted my path, where I held fear, and where Spirit was guiding me forward. They became my teachers, my compass, and my constant reminder that I was seen and loved.

A Vision That Changed Everything

On November 20, 1970, as I read "Black Elk Speaks," the room filled with blinding light. I felt hands press gently on my shoulders, holding me still as scenes of my life. Moments of pain, shame, and judgment flashed like negative film.

Then the pressure lifted.

A radiant Spiritual Master appeared before me dressed in white deerskin, an eagle feather rising from his braided hair. Looking directly into my soul, he said, "You are not alone." Behind him stood a line of luminous beings stretching beyond sight.

In those few minutes, I understood that my dreams were not escapes. They were Divine contact—my lifeline to Spirit.

That knowing changed everything. And it is the greatest truth I want every soul to remember:

You are not alone, and your dreams are the voice of the Divine speaking directly to you.

The Second Art: Courting the Dreamtime

Dreams flourish when we treat them as sacred.

The second art is to honor the dreamtime as a lover, a ceremony, a return to the holy. Dreams speak both through story and sensation—through the emotions we feel upon waking. Those feelings are part of the message.

Dreams draw from the unconscious, the place where every experience is stored. They reveal what is ready to heal, what is seeking expression, and what the soul is calling us toward.

To receive dreams clearly, our bodies must be cared for. Rest is a spiritual practice.

1. Create a sacred sleep environment.
2. Hydrate to activate your electrical system.
3. Enter sleep with intention rather than exhaustion.
4. Upon waking, write everything you remember—even a color or a fragment.

The more you record, the more dreams will reveal.

And then, create space for the messages to unfold. Meditate, breathe, chant, or sit in silence. Dreamwork is a relationship. The more attention you offer, the stronger the connection becomes.

Being The One means treating your body as an altar and your dreams as holy communion.

The Third Art: Walking the Path of Compassion

Dreams often reveal the places within us that still ache for love. They bring to light old wounds, unconscious fears, and buried memories not to shame us, but to release us.

Dreams become transformative when we meet them with compassion.

The Dream That Gave Me My True Name

One month after my third husband died unexpectedly, I was drowning in grief yet yearning for a new identity, a rebirth. I asked the Dreamtime for guidance.

That night, I dreamt I was at a spiritual retreat, walking up a green hillside to a gathering of people who told me others were waiting for my blessing. As each person sat, I placed my hands on their heads and gave blessings as I did in waking life.

Upon waking, I saw a name flash in my mind. But it vanished before I could grasp it.

Later that day, as I delivered ceremonial art to clients, three different shop owners addressed me not by my name, but as "Spirithawk." At a spiritual gathering that evening, a man turned to me and said, "Oh, here's Spirithawk," without apology or correction:

I received the message.
I claimed my true name.

From that moment forward, my life shifted from powerlessness to purpose.

Compassion is the way we turn revelation into transformation. As we forgive ourselves and others, the dream space becomes clearer, more peaceful, more luminous.

The Fourth Art: Co-Creating With God Through Taking Action–Dream Manifestation

Dreams are not passive stories. They are invitations to co-create with Spirit.

Every dream contains potential—a blueprint waiting to be activated through intention and action. Some dreams require large steps; others simply want acknowledgment, a drawing, a journal reflection, or a slight shift in behavior.

We were made in the image of a Creator. Imagination is our divine inheritance. Dreams do not replace action—they inspire aligned action.

Dream manifestation is the sacred partnership between Divine vision and human willingness.

Being The One is not about wishing for miracles. It's about becoming the miracle through aligned action inspired by divine dreams.

The Fifth Art: Trusting the Mystery of God's Timing

Trust is the bridge between the dream world and waking life.

Some dreams make sense immediately. Others take weeks, months, or years to reveal their meaning. But every dream unfolds according to Divine timing.

A Warning, a Letting Go, and a Love Destined by Spirit

In 1999, longing for a true life partner, I practiced dream incubation, falling asleep with prayerful intention.

One night, while camping with a lover, I dreamt a helicopter crashed outside our tent. As fireballs exploded, a clear voice—God's voice—said, "If you don't stop this, you will lose the house of David."

I awoke feeling shaken and confused. I didn't know anyone named David. But I honored the dream and ended the relationship.

Six months later, I met a man at a storytellers' guild meeting. His name was David. One conversation led to a friendship, a home, a life, and a marriage now twenty-six years strong.

That's the beauty of divine communication—God speaks in eternity, not in a hurry. Trusting the mystery means surrendering to the unseen with faith that Spirit is always several steps ahead of us.

Sometimes Being The One means taking action before the mind understands. Trusting the Divine understands for you.

The Sixth Art: Living in Gratitude

The final art is gratitude. For the seen and unseen. For the waking and the dreaming. Gratitude is how we honor the language of God. Each dream, even the confusing ones, is a gift meant to guide our evolution.

I end each night and begin each morning with a prayer of thanks: "Thank You, Creator, for the messages you send through my dreams. Thank You for trusting me to interpret and live them."

When we live in gratitude, we are no longer blown by the winds of fate. Fate is no match for the undying wisdom and love God has for each and every one of us. Gratitude turns sleep into sanctuary, life into ceremony, and our every breath into a dialogue with the Divine. I am grateful when I can Be The One for even one other Soul on their journey through life.

Closing Reflections

The Soul Medicine Arts are more than teachings—they are a way of remembering who we truly are. When we honor our dreams as divine communication, we return to our original nature as co-creators with God. Each night becomes a classroom for the soul; each morning, an invitation to live the wisdom revealed.

When I think of dreamers who changed the world, I think of Harriet Tubman. After surviving a brutal injury, she gained the gift of prophetic dreaming. Those dreams guided her through forests, swamps, hiding places, and escape routes on the Underground Railroad. Her visions saved hundreds of lives.

If she could trust God's dreams with nothing but courage and faith, how can we doubt our own?

Dreams are the gold of the soul—divine guidance wrapped in mystery, carrying us toward healing, purpose, and destiny.

Being The One is awakening to the truth that we are never alone and that Spirit is always speaking through every dream, every symbol, every whisper of love.

When we listen, trust, and take aligned action, we become living prophecies—the dream fulfilled.

She Who Dreams with Soul

Awake, dear world, for she is coming. With her dreams, her courage, and her love. She is dreaming a new world from the inside out! Her dreaming and her brave acts to heal and redesign her inner life will be mirrored in the Universe. She is beautiful. She is strong. She is kind and brave. She is "She Who Dreams with Soul."

Dr. Diana Spirithawk, DSS, is a visionary guide in Dreamwork, women's healing, and spiritual transformation. Founder of Spirithawk Sanctuary for Soul Medicine Arts, she teaches the ancient art of dream interpretation as a profound dialogue with the Soul and the Divine. Through her workshops, ceremonies, and mentorship, she helps women reclaim inner wisdom, heal old wounds, and step boldly into their next empowered chapter of life.

A world-renowned ceremonial artist and lifelong storyteller, Diana's work weaves feminine wisdom with modern spiritual practice, opening pathways to self-awareness and awakening. She is a best-selling author and holds a Doctorate in Spiritual Science. Diana is dedicated to helping others discover the messages within their dreams—and the destiny within their souls.

"Your dreams are not separate from your life—they are the living map of your soul's unfolding."

Get Instant Access to **Spirithawk's Guide to Understanding Your Dreams** so that you can harness the wisdom of your dreams in your everyday life.

Go to ▶ DianaSpirithawk.com

DianaSpirithawk.com

Spirithawk@DianaSpirithawk.com

CHAPTER 11

BECOMING FINANCIALLY FREE: COMING HOME TO MYSELF

Maureen Cohen
Soulful Money Mentor

Becoming Financially Free: Coming Home to Myself

My own mistakes in my financial journey have inspired me to help others avoid them. I often say, "We are all One" because I deeply believe that every person carries a divine spark—a purpose, a knowing we are part of God, a light that guides us when we learn to trust it. My vision is that people experience being One with each other and with God, reconnecting with the truth that we were created for Health, Harmony, and true Prosperity. My mission is to help people unlock both time and wealth without sacrificing their soul.

To me, Financial Liberation is synonymous with Freedom—the freedom to live fully, to express who you really are, to love without fear, and to make decisions from a place of empowerment rather than survival. For years, I believed I was "too spiritual" to care about having money. I equated spirituality with needing nothing, wanting nothing, and expecting nothing. But beneath that belief, I wasn't free. I was restricting myself, limiting myself, and avoiding money rather than understanding it.

Nothing changed until I opened my heart to learning. When I invited mentors, teachers, and new perspectives into my life, everything shifted. I met people who lived in the beautiful balance of prosperity and purpose—people whose wealth didn't cost them their integrity or peace. Their example opened a doorway for me. As I learned and healed, something awakened inside me: a calling to teach others what I had discovered. Financial liberation is not just about numbers; it's about identity and alignment.

I've always had a natural curiosity about finances and "the numbers," even when I wasn't the one earning the income. But curiosity is different from taking responsibility and being educated—and that responsibility entered my life powerfully after my divorce. After thirty-three years of marriage, suddenly everything was on my shoulders: my income, my future, my security. I had to learn quickly, and I had to learn deeply.

My former husband and I had decided early on that I would stay home with our young son because daycare cost more than

I earned. What seemed logical at the time created a long-term pattern of financial dependence. For over three decades, I relied on him financially. I worked off and on, but I never built self-sufficiency. I didn't realize how much of my confidence and identity I had given away until I had to reclaim it.

Once I began earning again, rebuilding from the ground up, Covid hit. Work slowed, income dipped, and uncertainty shook everything. For the first time, I chose not just to let everything fall apart. Instead, I looked for guidance. I found a mentor and took a program called "Enough." Through that transformative experience, I learned that I had enough to live on, enough to breathe, enough to rebuild. For the first time ever, I felt financially safe not because of someone else, but because of my own decisions and God's provision. That realization changed everything.

Knowing I am enough and I have enough freed me. It opened a new space within me, a space where possibility lived. I began to explore new expressions of myself, not from fear, but from curiosity. I started a new business aligned with my purpose, partnering with a company that provided the training, the tools, and the faith-based foundation I needed to flourish. This is the New Art of Living.

My commitment to becoming financially free has shaped every choice since. Interestingly, my divorce, which felt like a breaking point, ended up protecting me. Shortly after the divorce, my former husband filed for bankruptcy. Had we stayed married, I would have been pulled under financially as well. Instead, I was legally separate and able to preserve what I had earned. Sometimes God delivers us long before we understand the blessing.

The divorce also gave both of us room to grow. We had been stuck in patterns that no longer supported who we were becoming. Time apart offered healing, growth, and perspective. Today, we are good friends, which is a testament to maturity, forgiveness, and God's grace.

One piece of wisdom I share with everyone I teach is this:

Find a practice that brings you home to yourself.

Life will pull you, shake you, distract you, and challenge you. What matters is how quickly you can return to center. For some, it's prayer. For others, meditation, yoga, writing, or movement. For me, it is giving Light, a spiritual energy practice that connects me instantly to God. When I give Light, clarity returns. My next steps reveal themselves. Peace enters my body. And I remember God first—always.

"God First" is more than a motto for me. It's a compass. When I put God first, everything else falls into place. When I forget, everything becomes tangled. My life has taught me over and over again that we are never too old to begin anew. Never too old to rise. Never too old to become who we were meant to be.

My journey—through marriage, divorce, bankruptcy protection, spiritual awakening, self-reinvention, and financial rebuilding—has taught me that liberation is a process of returning to the truth inside us. And now, my purpose is to help others experience the same freedom.

Financial liberation is not just about bank accounts. It is about trust.

It is about faith.

It is about remembering that you are The One—the creator of your future, the steward of your resources, and the channel through which God works.

When you embrace that truth, your entire life transforms.

Closing Reflection: Coming Back to Your True Self

Take a moment to breathe.

Place your hand over your heart.

Feel the warmth, the presence, the quiet knowing inside you.

Ask yourself:

- Where in my life have I given away my power?
- Where am I ready to reclaim responsibility?
- What belief about money or worthiness no longer serves me?
- What would financial freedom feel like—emotionally, spiritually, physically?

You are not starting from nothing.

You are starting from wisdom, experience, and God's guidance.

Everything you have walked through has prepared you for what comes next.

You, too, are The One.

And the moment you decide to come home to yourself, your liberation begins.

Stepping Into Financial Strength: Your Next Chapter of Empowerment

As I continued my own healing and rebuilding, I realized something profoundly important: spiritual alignment and emotional grounding are essential—but they are only part of freedom. True liberation also requires practical wisdom, especially when it comes to money. For decades, I avoided financial matters because I didn't feel capable or confident. I let someone else handle everything, not realizing that my lack of financial education was keeping me dependent and vulnerable.

Once I began learning how money truly works—how protection, planning, and smart decisions create stability—everything shifted. I didn't just regain confidence. I regained authority over my life. I finally understood that God doesn't just want us to be spiritually strong—He wants us to be financially protected, prepared, and prosperous.

That realization is the core of the work I now do.

Today, my mission is to help others build the kind of financial confidence and security that creates peace of mind. I partner with a values-driven company that educates, equips, and empowers individuals to protect their families, prepare for emergencies, and create long-term financial freedom. I teach what I wish someone had taught me decades earlier:

Financial education is not optional.

It is protection.

It is stewardship.

It is self-respect.

And it is never too late to learn.

Where to Begin: Key Areas to Strengthen Your Financial Well-Being

If you are ready to step into greater financial clarity and confidence, here are a few essential practices to start with—the same ones that transformed my own life:

1. **Know your current financial reality.**
   Look honestly at your income, expenses, debt, and protection gaps. Awareness is power.
2. **Protect before you grow.**
   Before you invest or expand, make sure your income and family are protected through insurance, savings, and emergency planning.
3. **Get educated—truly educated.**
   Most schools don't teach financial literacy. Seek mentors, tools, workshops, and information that empower you to make informed decisions.
4. **Understand the difference between assets and liabilities.**
   Not everything that looks "prosperous" contributes to your future. Learn what actually builds wealth and what drains it.
5. **Create more than one stream of income.**
   Security comes from options. Explore opportunities aligned with your values that allow you to create predictable income beyond a paycheck.
6. **Make decisions from clarity, not fear.**
   When you pause, breathe, and return to center, you will always choose more wisely—in life and in money.
7. **Remember: money is spiritual.**
   Every dollar is energy. Every financial choice reflects what you believe you deserve. When you align your finances with faith and purpose, prosperity flows more naturally.

The Invitation

If my story resonates with you—if you, too, are ready to reclaim your confidence, your stability, and your God-given ability to create a secure future—I invite you to learn what I learned. You don't have to walk this road alone. Just as I found guidance when I needed it most, I now extend that same guidance to you.

You are capable.
You are worthy.
And you are ready.

Your next chapter of financial freedom begins the moment you decide to learn, grow, and protect what matters most. When you put God first and step forward with intention, your financial future becomes a place of peace—not fear—and possibility becomes your new normal.

Maureen Cohen is a soulful money mentor helping individuals and couples unlock time and wealth while staying true to their values. Inspired by hard-earned life lessons, she connected with the creators of the "New Art of Living"—a philosophy blending money mastery, self-improvement, and spiritual truth. Through practical strategies like 10% savings, multi-handed income, and personalized insurance policies, Maureen guides families to protect what matters, build legacy wealth, and live with more joy and less stress. Her ideal clients are individuals, as well as couples, raising children who are ready to make informed, empowering financial choices.

Maureen's vision is bold and beautiful: a world where people remember we are One—with each other and with God—and live in alignment with our divine design of Health, Harmony, and true Prosperity.

Whether through conversations, workshops, or customized coaching, Maureen is passionate about helping others rise above financial fear and live more freely.

Get instant access to "Empowering Families with The New Art of Living" and learn how you and your family can be transformed through The New Art of Living.

MaureenCohen.com

Maureen@MaureenCohen.com

Chapter 12

Bold Moves, Brave Faith: My Journey from Success to Significance

Lisa L. Baker
Founder | Coach | Speaker

Bold Moves, Brave Faith: My Journey from Success to Significance

My story begins in a small house with big dreams. Neither of my parents finished grade school, yet they taught me lessons no classroom ever could. I was the youngest of eight children, and only the second to graduate from college. Walking across that stage wasn't just about a diploma; it was proof. Proof that the story you inherit doesn't have to be the story you live. That possibility can become reality.

Trying to Fit In

When I started my career in financial services, I often found myself as one of the very few women in the room and, more often than not, the only Black professional. The environment was largely old, white, and male. The unspoken message was clear: You don't belong here unless you learn to fit in.

So, I tried.

I studied the rules, even the ones no one said out loud. Dress for success. Keep your head down. Work twice as hard, and maybe it will be enough. I wore the "shoulds" like armor, believing they would earn me a seat at the table. Armor keeps you safe, but it doesn't make you brave. And what I needed—though I didn't know it yet—was the courage to live by faith.

And to some degree, it worked. I did well. Leaders recognized my potential, gave me opportunities, and my career flourished. But underneath, I never fully shook the sense that I was an outsider.

The Breaking Point

Then came the day that changed everything.

I had been at Microsoft for seven years when a new Regional Vice President joined. In my very first one-on-one meeting with him, he looked straight at me and said, "Lisa, I didn't ask the team, but if I had asked who is the person who adds the least value, I'm sure they would have said you."

I was stunned. Just the year before, I had been promoted. I had never received a negative review. Yet here I was, being told I was worthless.

I decided right then: I'll prove him wrong.

But my second meeting with him was worse than the first. He drew a nine-block grid on the whiteboard: performance on one axis, potential for promotion on the other. Then, without hesitation, he put me in the bottom-left corner—low performance, low potential.

I broke. Tears blurred my vision before I even realized I was crying. I fought to hold it together, but the harder I tried, the faster they fell. I wasn't crying about the job. It was anger at his arrogance and grief that I had to navigate so much on my own. It was the release of everything I couldn't hold in anymore. On top of the stress at work, I was also going through a divorce and facing a financial crisis. His judgment landed on a weary soul already carrying more than it could hold.

A Bold Move Toward Freedom

What felt like the end turned out to be a bright new beginning.

I remembered a sermon I had heard many times about the Israelites asking the Egyptians for what they needed for their exodus from Egypt. For the first time, it struck me personally: Ask for what you need to be free.

So, I did.

I went to HR with a bold request. Eliminate my role. Sever me from the company and honor the severance policy. Move the contractor who reported to me into my position permanently.

I framed it as a win for everyone. The Regional VP would get what he wanted—me gone. The contractor would gain stability and recognition. And I would gain the freedom to walk away from an environment that no longer valued me. Asking for severance wasn't a desperate act; it was a bold move powered by brave faith.

To my surprise, they said yes. And I already had another opportunity lined up before my last day at Microsoft.

That moment taught me something I carry to this day: don't twist yourself into a mold that was never made for you. If the place you're in doesn't see your worth, don't change yourself. Change your environment. Go where you're celebrated. Don't stay where you're merely tolerated.

My very next boss at Synchrony later told me that hiring me was the best decision he'd ever made. I hadn't changed. The only difference was that I was finally in a place where I could thrive as myself.

Choosing Authentic Leadership

That experience changed me. I stopped leading to prove myself to people whose opinions held no real weight. Instead, I started leading with purpose—in service to those who matter most. I let go of the "shoulds" and gave myself permission to be my full, authentic self.

And when I did, my career took off.

At Synchrony, I spent a decade taking on roles with increasing responsibility. For the last three years, I served as Senior Vice President and General Manager of a $2.5 billion credit portfolio. Before that, I led another portfolio, growing it from $600 million to over $1 billion. In my first year as a General Manager, my team delivered award-winning results, including Portfolio of the Year, Sales Team of the Year, and Most Valuable Portfolio.

Through those experiences, I became known for building diverse, high-performing teams and cultivating cultures where people could bring their best. But achievement without fulfillment eventually wears thin. Even at the height of success, something inside still whispered: This still isn't it.

When Success Isn't Enough

On paper, I had all the markers of success—the executive title, the compensation package, the recognition. But truthfully, none of that was significant. Yes, I was successful. But I wasn't fulfilled by helping a massive corporation get even bigger.

So, I made another bold move.

I accepted a voluntary severance package (during a global pandemic) at the peak of my career. Making a leap without a clear plan wasn't like me. I value security. I was engaged at the time, and my fiancé—now my husband—hadn't signed up to be the sole breadwinner. My mother had raised me with a strong sense of independence. She told me to "stay in school, get a good education, so you don't ever have to depend on a man." Yet when I told him I felt like God was leading me to take the package, he was steady and supportive. He simply said, "If you truly believe God is calling you to this, go for it."

Then came the hopeful—and the naysayers.

The hopeful said, "I don't think they'll just let you leave. I bet they'll try to retain you." They wanted to believe that surely Synchrony would keep the highest-ranking Black female in the company. They held out hope that since there were so few Black executives, the company would go to extraordinary lengths to retain me. But I knew better. No matter your title, no one is irreplaceable.

The naysayers were louder. Colleagues and even friends questioned why I would walk away from such a lucrative career, especially when things were going so well. "Why would you leave now? You've worked too hard to get here." Their doubts echoed those that I didn't dare speak. I asked myself, "Is this Lisa, or is this the Lord? What am I going to do?" I had more questions than answers, but I leaned on prayer, faith, and the voices of my supporters.

"Faith is the substance of things hoped for, the evidence of things not seen." (Hebrews 11:1) This was truly a leap of faith—not a blind leap, but one rooted in lived experience. I had a history with God—a track record of grace I could trust. And that gave me the courage to bet on myself.

Becoming a Coach, Building Ascentim

On the other side, I found clarity. What I loved most about leadership wasn't the numbers or the accolades. It was the people.

The privilege of walking alongside leaders and teams—helping them grow, believe in themselves, and thrive.

That realization gave birth to my passion project, Ascentim, an award-winning coaching and leadership development practice.

Today, I help leaders break free from the relentless pressure to perform and discover the deeper purpose that fuels authentic leadership. I guide them through transformation—from pressure to purpose, from success to significance, so they lead boldly and live fully.

I know what it feels like to carry the weight of "not enough." I know what it's like to cry behind closed doors while pretending you have it all together. And I know the freedom that comes when you finally choose to lead as yourself.

That's why I do this work, so that it doesn't have to be as hard or lonely for the next leader as it was for me.

Your Next Move

Are you feeling it, too? The need for a shift in what you're doing or how you show up? Perhaps you're ready to stop doing and start becoming who you're meant to be.

Here are three clear signs that it may be time for you to make a bold move:

- You've outgrown your environment—and you can feel it in your bones. Are you hearing phrases like, "You're too much," "You're being dramatic," or "If I were you..."? If so, the role, the culture, and even the relationships around you no longer reflect the person you are becoming. You may have started shrinking to stay comfortable. But you're losing yourself in the process. And deep down, you know you're not too much; the environment is too small.
- Your success isn't as meaningful as you expected. Success has a strange way of disappointing. You work hard, hit the milestones, collect the titles, and still feel empty. On the outside, everything looks picture-perfect. On the inside, it doesn't add up. Saying that out loud feels risky because people might think you're ungrateful. But it's not

ingratitude. It's the truth that you were made for more. Your purpose is yet to be fulfilled.

- You feel a persistent tug. There's a quiet, persistent pull toward purpose. At times, it may feel faint, but you know it's there. It shows up in the pauses between meetings, in the sighs at the end of the day, and in the questions you can't quite articulate. You've tried to silence it with logic, loyalty, or busyness, but it keeps returning—asking you to listen, to trust, and to take action.

If any of this feels familiar, you're not alone. And you're not broken. You're standing at the edge of a bold transition, being invited into something more significant.

And I've created something just for you. It's a short teaching called ***Bold Moves: 4 Steps to Break Barriers and Build Confidence***, where I share what it really takes to break through and move from success to significance.

Titles fade. Accolades gather dust. What endures is purpose. And the boldest move of all? Choosing—every day—to lead with brave faith and live as who you truly are.

Lisa L. Baker is the Founder of Ascentim—an award-winning executive coaching and leadership development firm that helps high-achieving professionals and entrepreneurs lead boldly and live fully by discovering their unique Area of Greatness.

With over two decades in Fortune 500 leadership roles at Citigroup, Microsoft, and Synchrony, Lisa brings the rare ability to blend high-level strategic thinking with heart-led coaching that sparks sustainable growth. Her whole-person, inside-out approach is grounded in emotional intelligence and powered by her signature I.G.R.O.W. Framework, delivering measurable transformation for leaders, teams, and organizations.

Lisa equips high performers to quiet self-doubt, reclaim their voice, and align professional success with personal fulfillment—transforming pressure into purpose with less grind, more growth. A member of the Forbes Coaches Council, her thought leadership centers on helping leaders shed the mold of "should" and step fully into who they're meant to be.

Her work earned recognition, including Inc. Best in Business, Globee® Woman-Owned Startup of the Year, and the Stellar Business Award. But Lisa's proudest moments come from witnessing her clients become the best version of themselves—achieving more than they thought possible.

Her core belief? "We all have an Area of Greatness where our strengths, passions, and purpose converge. When we lead from that extraordinary place, we are our most powerful, authentic selves."

Get Instant Access to ***Bold Moves: 4 Steps to Break Barriers and Build Confidence***, where Lisa shares what it really takes to break through and move from success to significance.

Go to ▶ Ascentim.com/boldmoves

Ascentim.com

LBaker@Ascentim.com

Conclusion

Now It's Your Turn to Be The One

If you have read this far, chances are something within you has stirred.

Perhaps a story reminded you of a moment in your own life. A decision you once made that changed everything. A whisper you listened to... or perhaps one you ignored at the time but now recognize with new clarity.

Those moments matter.

As you have seen throughout the pages of this book, the journey of Being The One does not unfold in perfect, predictable steps. It reveals itself through experiences, turning points, courageous decisions, and sometimes even through the moments when we hesitate and later grow from what we learn.

Every life is filled with these invitations.

Sometimes the whisper is gentle.

Sometimes it grows louder until it becomes impossible to ignore.

Being The One is simply the choice to listen. To trust that inner voice that nudges you toward growth, service, creativity, connection, or leadership. It is the willingness to take inspired action even when the path ahead is not fully visible.

The authors in this book did not set out to be extraordinary. They simply chose, at certain moments in their lives, to say yes to what was calling them forward.

And that same possibility exists for you.

Your life will continue to present moments that ask something of you. Moments that invite you to step forward, to reclaim a part of yourself, to take a courageous step, or to live your vision more fully.

When those moments come, may you pause long enough to recognize them.

May you trust the wisdom that speaks from within.

And may you remember that the journey of Being The One is not about perfection, it is about presence, courage, and the willingness to respond when life calls.

Listen for the whisper.
Trust what it asks of you.
And when the moment comes...
be willing to step forward and Be The One.

Acknowledgments

To the contributing authors, thank you for saying yes to this project, for showing up with open hearts, and for sharing your stories with honesty, vulnerability, and the courage to be visible. Your willingness to stand in your truth makes this book a powerful reflection of what it means to Be The One.

To my husband, Barry Auchettl, thank you for being my partner in every sense of the word. Your unwavering belief in me, your calm strength, and your deep listening are gifts I treasure every day. I'm so grateful to walk this journey with you.

To PeggyLee Hanson, thank you for your thoughtful editing, your attention to detail, and your gentle touch in helping shape this collection. Your support brought clarity, flow, and grace to the process.

This book is the result of shared vision, heart, and courage. I'm honored to walk alongside each of you.

With love and appreciation,
Nancy

Continue Your Journey

If these stories have inspired you, I invite you to continue exploring the principles, practices, and community that support living and leading as The One.

Below you will find resources and opportunities designed to help you deepen your growth, expand your impact, and connect with others who are also answering the call.

Explore the next steps of your journey here:

1. **Deepen Your Practice: Read The One Philosophy Book.**
   This is the foundation. The principles shared in this book are rooted in The One Philosophy: six simple, yet life-changing principles that will guide you to lead with love, integrity, and vision. If you haven't read the full book yet, now's the time. It will deepen your understanding and amplify your impact.

☛ Get your copy at TheOnePhilosophy.com/

2. **Get Clarity: Take the "What's Your Impact Readiness Score?" Quiz.**
   Curious how ready you are to lead boldly and live your vision? This quick and insightful quiz will reveal where you excel and where you're being called to grow. Awareness is the first step to expansion.

☛ Take the quiz now at NancyMatthews.com/Ready

3. **Work With Me: Let's Explore What's Possible Together.**
   If you're ready to expand your leadership, your income, and your impact, and do it with joy, alignment, and ease, I'd be honored to support you. Whether it's through private coaching, masterminds, retreats, or speaking engagements, let's connect and explore the next best step for you.

☛ Contact me here at NancyMatthews.com/Contact

Your Story Matters

As you've seen throughout this book, every story has the power to inspire, encourage, and awaken something within others.

The authors who contributed to *Being The One: How to Lead Boldly and Live Your Vision – Volume II* each had moments in their lives when they listened to the whisper within and chose to take inspired action. Their willingness to share those experiences now allows others to see what is possible in their own lives.

Perhaps as you read these chapters, you recognized pieces of your own journey.

A moment that changed everything.
A challenge that revealed unexpected strength.
A decision that altered the direction of your life.

Those experiences matter.

Stories have always been one of the most powerful ways we learn, connect, and grow. When someone is willing to share honestly about their journey, it gives others permission to explore their own.

If you feel called to share your story of courage, transformation, faith, leadership, or personal awakening, I would love to hear from you.

The *Being The One* anthology series continues to grow, bringing together voices from around the world who are committed to living with intention and inspiring others through their experiences.

If you sense that your story may be part of a future volume, I invite you to explore the opportunity to contribute.

Learn more about contributing to a future volume:

👉 Nancy Matthews.com/author-apply

Sometimes the story you've lived becomes the inspiration someone else has been waiting for.

With infinite love and belief in you,
Nancy Matthews
Visionary • Mentor • Messenger of The One Philosophy

About Nancy Matthews

Nancy Matthews is a globally recognized speaker, author, and business advisor known as *The Culture Catalyst*, the one who bridges the gap between head and heart, profit and purpose, vision and reality.

She is the creator and author of *The One Philosophy*, a transformational mindset and movement built on a simple yet powerful idea: **What if we treated every person we meet as The One**? Since its release in 2013, this message has inspired individuals and organizations around the world to lead with love, live with vision, and build lives of deeper meaning and greater impact. In 2023, Nancy released the **10th Anniversary Edition**, celebrating a decade of influence and recommitting to the power of living and leading with intention.

Known for her ability to spark lasting change, Nancy teaches that when you embody *The One Philosophy*, everything around you improves:

- Relationships deepen through greater empathy and understanding
- Teams experience higher engagement, productivity, and trust
- Leaders inspire loyalty and innovation through authentic relationships
- Communities grow stronger through compassion and collaboration

Nancy is CEO of **Visions In Action** and Co-Founder of the acclaimed **Women's Prosperity Network**, an international organization that has empowered thousands of women to succeed in business and life. Her work has been featured alongside legends such as Jack Canfield, Les Brown, and Bob Burg, and in 2024, she was honored with the **Presidential Lifetime Achievement Award** for her service and dedication to uplifting humanity.

Whether through her books, stage presence, or mentoring programs, Nancy inspires people to **lead boldly, live their vision, and Be The One**, for themselves and for others.

She is also a philanthropist, devoted wife and life partner, proud mother, loving sister, and a great friend. Her journey is a living example of what's possible when we trust our inner knowing, take aligned action, and show up with love and purpose.

To learn more about Nancy's work, explore The One Philosophy, or invite her to speak, visit:

- NancyMatthews.com
- TheOnePhilosophy.com
- Nancy@NancyMatthews.com

Made in the USA
Coppell, TX
09 June 2026

80013283R00075